THE GREAT MOTION PICTURE SOUNDTRACK ROBBERY

An Analysis of Copyright Protection

BY

KEN SUTAK

Archon Books   1976

Library of Congress Cataloging in Publication Data

Sutak, Ken, 1948–
  The great motion picture soundtrack robbery.

  "A large part of this book first appeared in the Bulletin of the Copyright Society of the U.S.A., 22:5 (June 1975)"
    Includes bibliographical references and index.
    1. Copyright—Moving pictures, Talking—United States. 2. Copyright—Moving-picture music—United States. 3. Copyright—Phonorecords—United States. I. Title.
KF3070.S8   346′.73′0482   75-43626
ISBN 0-208-01580-9

© 1975, 1976 by Ken Sutak
Published 1976 as an Archon Book,
an imprint of The Shoe String Press, Inc.,
Hamden, Connecticut 06514

All rights reserved

Printed in the United States of America

A large part of this book first appeared in the *Bulletin of the Copyright Society of the U.S.A.*, 22:5 (June 1975), and permission of the Society to reproduce this material is gratefully acknowledged

To my parents,
 Gilda Sutak Simpson
  and Richard Simpson

CONTENTS

	Introduction	ix
	The Great Motion Picture Soundtrack Robbery	3
I.	The Soundtrack Copyrightability Conflict	5
II.	Toward an Affirmation of Soundtrack Copyrightability	25
III.	Motion Picture Soundtrack Piracy	80
	Conclusion	102
	Glossary of Legal Terms	105
	Table of Cases	107
	Index	109

INTRODUCTION

In reach and ambition, copyright law springs from a single bold premise: protection of "authors," by way of protection of their "writings," benefits society by insuring an ever-expanding production of those creative works which spin and sometimes lodge in the center of society's culture.

The terms "authors" and "writings" are those employed in the Copyright Clause of the United States Constitution. As legal terms, they have long since ceased to be very controversial. "Authors" are the originators, the creators, of "writings," and "writings" are those literary, dramatic, and musical works which we associate, in nonexclusive fashion, with art, education, and entertainment. However, the copyright premise itself, and a *system* of copyright which wields such a premise as an intellectual sword, have never ceased to be anything but controversial. Nor have these parent controversies ever emerged fully defined.

Part of the problem of definition arises because the copyright premise and the functional copyright system are grounded rather elusively in what has been called "the metaphysics of the law." The phrase was coined by Justice Joseph Story, who served on the United States Supreme Court from 1812 until 1845; he offered it as a description of copyright itself. It is a strange and malleable country, this metaphysical land of the law. Its borders originate in time and its inhabitants are largely metaphorical, ranging from heroes to villains, gods to devils, saints to witches, hosts of angels to phalanxes of demons. At one time or another, all of these emblematic subjects have been conjured up and called upon by courts and commentators when confronting a particular, or especially a generic, copyright controversy. As a result of this emotional interest invariably brought to copyright investigations, copyright itself has come to be considered one of the most fascinating intellectual arenas offered in and by The Law. The law, however, sometimes acts as if it hasn't yet comprehended the nature of the war that has been raging within the one legal arena reserved for metaphysical combat.

To be sure, the courts and the commentators have not been alone in their willingness, when confronting copyright, to pay homage to figures born largely of fantasy, less largely of vision. The point very much worth making as preface to a study of a particular twentieth-century copyright problem is that this legal philosophization of copyright has been quite responsible *directionally*: that it is, in fact, a proper way to go about plumbing the blessings and evils which attach to creative acts and the systematic dissemination of their fruit, which is to say, their commercialization. The genealogy of copyright being metaphysical, then, an introduction to one copyright problem of contemporary vintage shall be metaphysical as well, lest the accumulated metaphors of centuries of copyright debates go unacknowledged, their accelerated effects on contemporary copyright controversies left untouched.

Yet if metaphysics must provide the highway leading to one analytical station of copyright law, nothing said here need emerge as indefinite. Nor should anything metaphysical said here be taken as copyright scripture. If the legal analyst who approaches copyright has long had license to deal mythically with his subject, he has never been able to work with the weight of metaphorical agreement following seizure of the law's most romantic elective. If everything from god to devil, hero to villain, may be said to stand and flourish in the lay of copyright, no one mythic figure may be said to stand squarely in anything even approaching a universal legal vision. Copyright law intrigues courts and commentators because it is the one area of law to which the citizen as artist/educator/entertainer looks for a variety of protections, not the least of which is protection of *his* economic interests through protection of *his* work. But copyright law also befuddles courts and commentators because other interests are involved. Other considerations of benefit arise in the metaphysical landscape, such that social good and social harm rarely appear quite clear, and the mythic figures of right and wrong rarely appear satisfactorily aligned against each other.

The historical tendency upon the parts of courts and commentators has been not only to choose sides but to square the sides in accord with personal bias before choosing. This tendency probably is quite natural and even necessary, whatever its effects in a given instance upon the development of law and social behavior. What, after all, are angels and demons, heroes and villains, but projections of personal bias? And who can ever be free of that?

Not many courts, not many commentators, and not this writer. Though I have my own ideas about what our present Register of Copyrights, Barbara Ringer, has called "the demonology of copyright," I bring to the present work that which Ringer brought to her celebrated 1974 lecture: a high—but not an extreme—protectionist bias. Just what *that* is may

INTRODUCTION

best be gleaned by resurrecting our chief copyright lawyer's defining statement, for I do not think it can be improved:

> I believe it is society's duty to go as far as it can possibly go in nurturing the atmosphere in which authors and other creative artists can flourish. I agree that the copyright law should encourage widespread dissemination of works of the mind. But it seems to me that, in the long pull, it is more important for a particular generation to produce a handful of great creative works than to shower its schoolchildren with unauthorized photocopies or to hold the cost of a jukebox play down to a dime, if that is what it is these days.

The passage is from *The Demonology of Copyright* (separately published by the R. R. Bowker Company in 1974). The important thrust in this credo is, of course, "nurturing the atmosphere in which authors and other creative artists can flourish." There is more to effecting this goal than retaining protective copyright laws which are on the books. There is even more to seeing this goal realized than insuring that new protective copyright laws are enacted. There is, as always, the complex philosophical task of distinguishing heroes from villains. There is also, as something relatively new, the considerable physical task of putting the villains out of business.

As to the last, let there be no mistake about it: the villains are very much in business, and they operate in a fashion which allows the nomenclature of villainy to attach. Whatever the precise shapes and forms attributed to honorable and dishonorable forces through centuries of judicial and extrajudicial copyright debates, the state of this country's copyright law has for some time offered legal distinctions between copyright owners and copyright criminals. Irrespective of this institutional dichotomy, a full half of the present century has been an era in which the demonic figures of pre-twentieth-century copyright mythology have moved out of the romantic imaginations of copyright conversationalists and into the real world of copyright criminality.

The transformation has been slow, certainly. It may even be said that the bulk of the migration has occurred during the past decade. The response of copyright law, both at the federal level and at the state level, has been even slower to develop. In some quarters—the present work deals with but one—copyright law has produced no active opposition at all, despite entrenched defiance of illicit bent and statutory mandate of licit origin. So copyright law, by virtue of an impotency which derives solely from inertia, has become wedded to a criminal plague to which it now relates quite curiously, partly as silent victim, partly as permissive guardian. And the plague which has taken hold in the wake of the law's transmogrification has come to affect the general public just as detrimentally, though certainly more indirectly, as it continues to torture those creative interests more readily associated with a protectionist copyright law. Crime, at various economic levels and to overlapping commercial standards organized, has discovered the literary, dramatic, and musical "writings" of "authors," and others besides "authors" and their investors are paying the price.

That price embraces much more than the monetary value of stolen creative goods, but even in this form alone the cost is considerable. To cite only the two most notorious areas of copyright criminality in the United States, record piracy represents to the recording industry an aggregate domestic theft of $200 million each year, while the figures for film piracy in the motion picture industry have been estimated at annual levels ranging from $50 million to $200 million, with $100 million being at least a reasonably reliable quotation. The public pays its share of the losses in terms of lost taxable income, lost jobs, higher prices, and the cost of mounting opposition to the thievery. Thus, the demons which have long populated the metaphysics of the law have not only become physical, they have become very well paid, with the public paying part of their way.

What they have *not* become—yet, anyway—is perhaps the sharpest travesty of all. Few outside of law enforcement, the judiciary, the legislature, and the entertainment industry, are prepared to label record pirates, film pirates, or other pirates as criminals in the sense that bank robbers or street muggers are criminals. Part of the reason for this reluctance probably arises from the fact that copyright pirates are in business to serve the public creative goods which the public cannot obtain as cheaply or as expediently. And part of the reason probably derives from the fact that copyright pirates infringe property rights, at a time when property rights and personal rights are being called—in some quarters—two different things. But a fair slice of the explanation for this lapse in public judgment no doubt lies in the fact that we live in an era of publicized corporate crime, perceived corporate mendacity, and felt corporate greed. Copyright pirates prey in the first instance upon corporate property, and that, unfortunately, is too generally viewed today as held under a presumption of ill-gotten gain. That copyright pirates cannot steal from a corporation without also infringing and feeding upon the rights and interests of our "authors" and the public itself is a fact of copyright criminality which tends to escape general attention. *Some* corporations are

INTRODUCTION

getting theirs, and for too many who have felt a corporate bite or two, that's enough, that's all there is to it.

But it isn't. It is not enough of a rationalization to justify property expropriation, and property expropriation, even if it be called property redistribution, is not all there is to it. Copyright criminality is serious criminality for the most severe and the most subtle of moral and economic reasons, and that it has taken so long for such a unique form of larceny to be officially treated as serious criminal behavior in *any* area of copyright protection has brought us to the very edge of an Armageddon in affairs of American copyright.

For if copyright in the twentieth century has witnessed the arrival of genuine villains upon the metaphysical landscape of the law, within the same arena copyright has also presided over the creation of genuine heroes. The twin births have been by virtue of a redefinition of those concepts copyright theologians of centuries past dressed in the philosophical apparel of saints and witches, never dreaming that their cosmic inventions would take flight from legal imagination to light upon a century so technological as the twentieth, and to set upon a society so technologized as our own.

Yet, if the transmigration has come to pass, it remains to be explained. I think I know a little about what has happened, and about the dynamics, both legal and philosophical, that have produced a generic copyright crisis today and which will decide a variety of collisions between *pro*copyright and *anti*copyright forces tomorrow. I think that the interplay of these dynamics during this century has had and will continue to have a profound impact on American life, and I think that an explanation of how and why that is so may first be traced to the country's origin itself.

America actually had domestic copyright statutes on its law books before the country had a constitution. The difficulty with these early copyright laws was that they were of state origin and failed to provide effective national protection to intangible intellectual property which could cross state borders more easily than a chattel. These local laws, limited in their separate effects to the boundaries of the separate enacting states, had been adopted by all of the original thirteen states except Connecticut and Delaware under the Articles of Confederation which held the states together before the adoption of the Constitution.

This lack of national copyright protection was slated for correction by James Madison in his address to the Constitutional Convention in April, 1787, on the subject of "The Vices of the Political System of the United States." The desirability of national protection for intellectual property seems to have been accepted at first and full impression by both the Convention and the states adopting the Constitution. Thus arrived Article I, Section 8, Clause 8 of the United States Constitution, which reads: "The Congress shall have power... To promote the Progress of Science and useful Arts, by securing for limited Times to Authors and Inventors the exclusive Right to their respective Writings and Discoveries." The first federal copyright act enacted pursuant to this power, extending statutory protection to authors of books, maps, and charts, was signed into law by President George Washington on May 31, 1790.

Following Madison's "Vices" speech to the Constitutional Convention and prior to Washington's approval of the first national copyright act, Madison himself had had more to say about the federal power to extend copyright protection. The following is from *The Federalist Papers, No. 43*:

> The utility of this power will scarcely be questioned. The copyright of authors has been solemnly adjudged in Great Britain to be a right of Common Law. The right to useful inventions seems with equal reason to belong to the inventors. The public good fully coincides in both cases with the claims of individuals. The states cannot separately make effectual provision for either of the cases, and most of them have anticipated the decision of this point by laws passed at the instance of Congress.

Now, the words ring with neither the fervor of the nationalistic sage nor the passion of the literary adventurer. But Madison certainly was a bit of both, and underlying his concise argument was a concern for encouraging native authorship through a *moral* system of copyright, one which would reflect the ideals of human liberty for which the Revolution had been fought, upon which the Constitution was to be based, and to which Madison had committed his soul. Since the moral fabric of this system is subtle, and as the moral nature of copyright has much to do with the assault on copyright today, it is worthwhile to look more closely at what Madison was talking about, at what he in large degree viewed as axiomatic.

He was, in the first instance, talking about property, which is a legal concept describing a specific matter of personal right. He was also talking about the public good, which is not so much a legal concept describing a communal right as it is a utilitarian consideration achieved through the extension of a social benefit to a society which, through its legal institutions, defines specific matters of personal right. Further, Madison was speaking about the weight and influence of two kinds of law, common and statutory, both of which originated not in America but in England. And lastly he was talking about power, specifically the power of statutory law to affect common law, and thereby to affect both the personal right of property and the public good. From the interaction and manipulation of these forces—all quite conceptual, all somewhat political, all very real—emerged the various federal copyright laws of the United States, which were to become in the twentieth century the Copyright Act of the United States.

How so? Consider first the abstract matter of property. An author, whatever his field, hammers out an intellectual production by placing upon the anvil of his mind whatever raw data he has been able to draw from the forge of worldly experience. The process may or may not involve the expenditure of alternate opportunities and prodigies of stamina, time, courage, love, faith, and commitment. In any case, the author is likely to feel that what he has produced should be and is *his*, and few who see him emerge successfully from the deep will be ready to disagree with his claim of ownership.

Though the earliest supportive historical evidence is ancient enough to be slim, we may take it on instinct that the general willingness to accept the author as at least some kind of property owner originates in pastoral/agrarian, venatic/military, and even religious analogies. Like the earliest shepherds and farmers who toiled upon the earth, the author struggles to nurture a living thing. If it comes into being, we see it as the product of his care and therefore his own. This is the motif that once led an ancient Irish monarch, King Diarmed, to settle a question of property ownership in a manuscript with a simple statement of natural law: "To every cow its calf." This aphorism does not stand alone, however; just as the early hunter brought down the beast, just as the old warrior won his triumph in the test of combat, the successful author consummates what to him is the necessary hunt, he fights and wins what to him is the good fight. The search may have taken him through a maze of personal dangers, and the combat may have been waged with a host of private demons, but if good King Diarmed could never have laid claim to an Irish crown by excusing himself from personal confrontation with danger or demon, certainly the author may lay claim to property when he enters and emerges victoriously from the private fray. And if the author takes from the earth and gives back, if he manufactures or accepts his own adversity and swallows that adversity in will, we tend to feel that he has come close to the godhead. For he is then creator, and subject of the claim, made as early as the sixteenth century by a French lawyer on behalf of a writer, that just as God possesses the heavens and earth as works of his word, so, too, an author is master of his creation.

Undeniably, there are both moral and romantic senses of natural justice imbedded in these equations. But the emphasis in such justice may be said to shift to the moral aspect rather than to the romantic one, for the romanticism here involved is attached to historical considerations of social efficiency. The products of the soil and the herd fed the farmer and shepherd and allowed them to live off of their toil. The prize of the hunt went to the hunter and the spoils of the combat went to the victor because these were survival operations wherein the fittest survived. A power that could decree that the author was master of his creation could also invoke the same principle of natural justice to assert autocratic sovereignty on earth in the name of an original creator through whom political rule could be claimed. Thus, even the earliest historical analogies supporting a notion of property right in authorship were never without their communal implications. If the author as toiler, as man of private adventure, as creator, was to accept the benefit of natural justice, he would also have to reckon with its reach.

Enter the public good. It is not always very public; it is not always or entirely a good; and the considerations which it subsumes are not always harmonious. But copyright arguments on behalf of the public good are almost as old as copyright arguments in favor of a private property right, and where the latter have gone, the former have followed, sometimes ferociously. After all, the act of authorship is a process of discovery, one which may extend anywhere from the private self to the public soul. It is good for a society to have members who embark upon the intellectual tides of creative discovery. Therefore, it is in the interests of society to encourage this kind of embarkation in those who have the inclination to shove off and the ability to stay afloat. Still, nothing well-achieved is achieved easily, creative discovery least of all. The voyage being much less than simple, the encouragement must be much more than slight.

However, discovery without dissemination will rarely benefit the discoverer very much, and it won't benefit society at all. If it is good for a society to have authors, it is primarily because their work may be presented to society. The presentation involves two things of great value to society: access and use. Access to the creative discovery works to the public good because it allows society to learn what may not have been known before, to reclaim what may have been earlier lost, to think of or to feel what may not have been widely thought of or felt before, to develop new creative discoverers who may not have been drawn to creative discovery before. Use of the creative discovery works to the public good because it allows new creative discoverers to employ the creative discovery as raw data in the pursuit of new and different creative discoveries.

On the other hand, this presentation so valuable to society involves two things of great danger to the author: theft and loss of control. Theft subsumes plagiarism and piracy, the former being a public denial of the author's achievement (for the plagiarist will publicly claim credit himself), the latter being a correctly credited public copying of the author's achievement which threatens the author's ability to receive his rightful income (for the pirate expropriates much or even all of the income generated by the achievement). Loss of control over the creative discovery involves the author's loss of any say about what is done with his work in any medium, including the one in which he originally presented his work, and whether or not he is paid for the unauthorized transformation.

Now, in the most abstract and immediate of economic terms, theft of the author's creative discovery and loss of the author's control over the forms by which his creative discovery will be disseminated do not erode the public good. In the same coldly calculated terms, the public good may even be said to be enhanced. After all, the creative discovery has settled upon society such that access and use are not only confirmed but rampant. The author's work thereafter continues to be disseminated throughout society; further, it is disseminated in any form anyone wishes to deliver; and it is available in all quarters but the originating one more cheaply than it is available from the author.

However, when these economic terms are expanded from abstraction and immediacy to encompass not only moral considerations but also economic terms stretched full circle, it becomes apparent that such a social bargain must explode under its own weight so as to eradicate the public good here involved. If the author is accorded no property rights in his creative discovery, such that he will not be protected against theft and loss of control, matters of access and use will be academic: the author simply will either not create or not present to society what he does create, because nothing should be given to a society prepared to offer only the devil in return. Moreover, unless the property rights accorded the author are substantial, many of the best and the bravest authors still will not create or present to society what is created, because nothing still need be given to a society prepared to offer too much of the devil in return. In either case, if the call to create remains firm, there will be other societies ready to compete with greater hospitality for the author's presence.

On the other hand, the fact that a bargain with the devil is impractical does not mean that a bargain cast solely on the side of the angels is practical. If the author is accorded too much of a property right in his creative discovery, or if he is given substantial property rights for too long a time, then matters of access and use may still be academic and they will certainly be at least strained: access will be minimal or very expensive, and use may be disallowed.

There was, then, a natural conflict in the matter of natural justice and its bearing upon the author. The resolution of this conflict came to lie in compromise, in a delicate balance between ownership rights in a chattel and ownership rights in air—great conflicting weights set at opposite ends of a metaphysical scale. And it fell to the law to devise the compromise, for what was the law if not adept at carefully setting opposing weights upon intricately invented scales?

The issue fell firstly into the lap of the common law. Common law is judge-made law, derived initially from innate human agreements in matters of good and bad, progressively from Judeo-Christian principles of right and wrong, and eventually from an integrated legal system which sees new laws expand harmoniously from a base composed of recorded judgments which have been passed previously. The earliest common law judges in England seem to have been no more prepared to deny the author his analogized rights as intellectual toiler, adventurer, and creator, than King Diarmed had been willing to deny the cow its calf. The author's creative production, being the result of his intellectual labor, was seen to be as much his property as any land or chattel which he owned, and his rights in his creative work were seen to be similarly absolute and perpetual. That is, his property rights in his creative work were so defined as long as he chose to exercise complete private control over his creative property. If he published his intellectual property—if, for instance, he distributed his manuscript for public consumption—other considerations would loom so as to affect his property rights in the creative work. A manuscript which he authorized or produced himself might still be *his*, but a manuscript which he did not authorize or produce himself, though identical with his own, might be something else. This might be claimed because the property rights in the former had been defined by the nature of toil, war, creation, and the hunt, while the property rights in the latter remained to be fathomed in terms of the communal implications of social efficiency which lay in the same endeavors.

The emerging divide in protection burst full flower with the invention of the printing press and movable type in the middle of the fifteenth century. For an ensuing period of roughly one hundred years, the author remained publicly unprotected from theft and loss of control of his work. At the same time, and then for another century and a half, piracy, plagiarism, and sheer literary butchery flourished in England.

Not until the early years of the eighteenth century did the rights of authors shift from common law chaos to statutory order—and if this jump passes from an era of English autocracy to a period of English democratic reform so as to leave unattended a gap filled with developments of possible relevance, their weight is nonetheless reserved for subsequent measure. The variant property rights of authors emerged from the depths of English common law to assume definitive shape within the Statute of Anne, an act passed by Parliament in 1710 and the first copyright statute in world history. Here at last the author stood as property owner within a system of noncensorial regulation built upon fundamentally democratic ideals. But the stance was unique, for the author now stood in the shadow of two lairs of law which operated as one system. And the property right which the author was recognized to possess was in fact a form of property deviating from the norm, for in matters of exclusive ownership it would take root as a function of use and thereafter be subject to the limits of time.

Under such a system, the author was still to retain an absolute and perpetual common law property right in his creative work—so long as he did not publish his creative work. If, however, the author did render his creative work unto the public by making it available for general consumption, whatever property right he enjoyed under common law ended. It could then be superseded by a statutory property right. The grant of this statutory property right was to be contingent upon the author's compliance with any procedural terms set down in the copyright statute. And the reach of this statutory copyright—the amount and the span of the protection accorded to the author—would only exist upon those terms established within the copyright statute. In other words, the government would grant continuance of and more elaborate protection to what it recognized to be a property right of authorship, but it would extract in return an accommodation to the public good.

Still, there would be no political usury involved, as under the Statute of Anne protection was never to be a matter of to the cow the calf, to the public the milk. If the author's creative productions were too valuable to society to remain free of regulation, the author himself was simply too precious to society to be exploited, too necessary for the cultural growth of society not to be greatly encouraged.

So the balance was laid within the law that the author might have a great property right for a while, and no property right at all after the while expired. For a limited time he would have an exclusive right in his creative work, he would have nothing less than a monopoly, he would be protected against all manner of theft, he would have absolute control over the paths by which his creative work might run to the public, and all that he would have in these respects for as long as he would have anything at all would be subject only to an amorphous understanding that other authors might make use of his creative work in fashioning new and different creative works of their own. Thus, the author would be attracted not only to discovery but to dissemination. Moreover, by virtue of so salient an attraction he would be hard put to pronounce the law a rogue. And if the public for a time was to pay the price of monopoly at the direction of the law, the public nevertheless would have the law to thank for seeing the creative goods delivered and afoot forever.

But the day would come—and it would be a reasonable day—when the author, his assigns, or his heirs would have nothing, for so much having been given by the law at an early hour, so much would be taken back by the law at a later time. Within this balance lay a bargain, a pact as honorable as any which had ever been made in the law. For it had been struck by reasonable men casting one analytical eye at the godhead and another analytical eye at the hellhound, and to their credit such men had perceived that each object of their vision bore traits of the other—that the author, the public, and the law would have to make do with something of each. What, then, had begun in considerations of natural justice had risen to the level of moral and profoundly communal affirmation. In all matters of copyright protection, the author, the public, and the law were now to be bound together in common interest and in common degree of promise to and claim upon each other. If there were to be those who would break the common faith, then they would have the author, the public, and the law to pay, and perhaps the devil as well.

Though there would be some in England who would deny a grand and intricate beauty in this resolution, upon another continent and near the end of the same century the author of *The Federalist Papers* would not deny it, nor would the framers of an American Constitution, nor the states of a new nation conceived upon principles even more democratic than those then operating in England. If the American people were to have their freedom defined in terms of personal rights and public responsibilities, then American authors would have to have their literary and artistic liberty defined in equivalent fashion. Since, in all basic copyright matters of personal right and public good, the English Statute of Anne provided not just the only model but a noble and democratic one, care was taken by the Constitutional Convention to insure that the world's first copyright statute would mother the world's second copyright statute, just as English common law was providing the foundation for American common law. The elected midwife was the Copyright Clause of the American Constitution, which in simple and direct terms spoke of federal legislative power to issue federal statutes granting to authors exclusive rights in their creative works for limited times, all for the promotion of the public good. Nothing in the ancestral balance was to shift, nothing in the ancestral bargain was to be eroded. All that was new was that a moral, communal affirmation of one country was to become a moral, communal affirmation of another country. In all matters of copyright protection, the American author, the American public, and American law were to be as commonly bound in depth of interest and in reach of interacting promise and claim as were their English antecedents.

And so, step by step, they were. The series of societal agreements began with a congressional grant of copyright protection to authors of books, maps, and charts in 1790, as noted earlier. It continued throughout the nineteenth century as Congress issued separate grants protecting authors of prints, authors of musical compositions, authors of dramatic compositions, authors of photographs, authors who painted, drew, or sculpted. The agreements were workable and they did work, producing in the long girth of an expansionist century not only native creative works but also distinctively American creators, willing to push beyond new frontiers of creative discovery just as the heroic ideal of nineteenth-century America lay in pushing the physical frontier of the nation into the waters of a western sea. In this pursuit the American author stood largely as metaphysical explorer, more often than not devoting his work to encouraging agrarian conquest by hard-living men and women capable of creating a pattern of heroic achievement within the polyglot civilization they sought to expand, not without excess, to a further doorstep of the continent itself. And if the country began to change as the conquest rushed toward conclusion, so the American author began to change. Like his counterpart embroiled in the civilization of the land, he began to show more and more the signs of the entrepreneur. As the century swept toward its end, it became clear that the law which nurtured the American author would have to change a bit also. In procedural matters the various copyright laws of the United States would have to be centralized, and in 1870 they were. In substantive reach and in common goal the same laws would have to be redrawn, expanded, and consolidated, and as soon as the nineteenth century was under the belt they were.

Yet the twentieth century looked to be something very different from the century which had passed. New technologies were appearing more swiftly and with greater weights of social power in their carriage than technologies had ever appeared before, and they were generating sweeping changes in patterns of American life. The physical frontier of the nation was closing, and in matters of national collective objective agrarian conquest was giving way to urban commercialization. Even as the heroic ideal of the nation was passing, a corporate ideal of less than universal psychological agreeability was rushing headlong to fix technological imperatives in the reflective currents of dream and destiny where agrarian imperatives had stood before meeting displacement.

This is not the moment to deal centrally with any one of these historical developments, but it may be the place to consider what effects these developments bore on the American author. He had, after all, been much involved in the life of the nation during the nineteenth century. What would be his place in the uncharted twentieth?

Certainly he would have his technological goals, just as he had always had some. I am not speaking here about goals of invention; invention brings into play patent considerations, not copyright ones. But if the author would not be interested in making machines, he might be interested in seeing them made, in seeing them look attractive, in seeing them sold, in seeing them used properly, or in seeing them understood fully. Yes, the author might never be the mother of invention, but he could prove valuable indeed as any one of an assortment of midwives. So the author stood in several respects as ally to technology, more prominently now than he had ever stood in this regard before. And if he did not welcome a position within the shadow of technology, he would have the freedom to step aside and to cast a shadow of his own making.

But what kind of freedom was this to be—and what manner of shadow? If the author naturally enough seemed to be a direct influence upon technology, just as naturally he looked to be directly influenced by technology. For among the new technologies there were certain to be technologies of vast communicative powers. Indeed, the phonograph and the motion picture had already arrived without clear-cut protective guidelines established for their use; they were now pushing the initial weight of their importance into the early moments of the twentieth century by virtue of discovery and rough-hewn commercial exposure during the closing moments of the nineteenth century. The potential—especially the commercial potential—for dissemination of the author's creative work suddenly appeared to be vast: more vast in some specifics than the framers of the American Constitution could ever have imagined, vaster still in many other specifics than men alive in the first decade of the twentieth century could even then perceive. Could the author be denied a freedom to take advantage of these new technologies, when he had been granted a freedom to take advantage of earlier technologies? Could he now be denied an absolute protection from theft and loss of control during the span of his property right, in the name of a public interest in dissemination—dissemination which could now be as widely cast as the broadening technological foundation of twentieth-century life would allow?

Yes: but it would take a constitutional amendment to allow the denial, and such an amendment could only be frightening to a democracy, ominous to a culture, and disruptive to a moral society. Though the Copyright Clause of the Constitution did not establish American copyright, since it only conferred upon Congress the power to establish American copyright if Congress wished to do so, the Copyright Clause did establish the basic rules by which American copyright was to be established if it was to be established at all. These rules were as locked to principles of personal liberty and public responsibility as were many other rules attached to other powers extended to Congress by the great document. If these rules were now to be put to the knife, the deadliest of democratic implications would rise through the tear: where next would legislative action in the name of majority benefit cut a path through minority freedom? The knifing itself would stand as precedent, the hilt of the metaphor beckoning a new hand: what other constitutional rules underlaid by notions of personal liberty and public responsibility would serve as later target?

And to what end the Copyright Clause as target, to what finish a constitutional amendment as knife? More than political implications would be born of the deed, because the deed would not promote the useful arts but rather retard the useful arts, assuming that the constitutional directive about promoting the useful arts would itself escape the knife, that promotion of the useful arts would remain a social desirée. But could this social ambition remain an active goal, could this constitutional instruction escape the knife for long, when a copyright system built upon a moral basis of communal agreement would be turned inside-out and ejected as a subset within a universal legal system, which itself had been morally based upon interlocking patterns of communal agreement, and with the erosion of the universe left hanging as the prime implication spun by the disintegration of the subset? No, the deed would be too great, the repercussions of the act would be too sinister; ripples of repressive effects not now planned stood to churn from entry into such waters. One could no more hack "exclusive Right" out of the Copyright Clause of the Constitution than one could rip "limited Times" from the same provision and know that the American public would not suffer by dint of the slash.

Besides: the author himself was gaining a new importance in American life—he was assuming new roles which stretched beyond any act of alliance with technology. It was not just that the nation could not stand as a land of opportunity or claim that it encouraged entrepreneurship if it offered the benefits and extracted the responsibilities of a seething capitalism to all but authors, who in the denial of procopyright treatment would stand only to be hamstrung by the law. No: if the frontier of the nation was about to close so as to place a territorial seal upon civilization, if technological imperatives were ready to be implanted in the nation's consciousness so as to breed the technologization of life in the new century, then by implication of these massive shifts the author would have to be allowed and encouraged to take contemporary flight with freedom intact, freedom even magnified. For technology bore the capacity to work good and evil—a capacity still incapable of definition but already unmatched—such that the seeds of technologization were sure to be seeds of new patterns of death as well as new patterns of life. Who would be afoot to disect twentieth-century mysteries of heaven and hell as yet incomprehensible, who would rise to inveigh against the most insidious reaches of technology if such reaches were extended, and who would be able to fight new battles in new arenas which contained new demons requiring the use of new weapons—if not the author?

Not, to be sure, the traditional American hero of the nineteenth and eighteenth centuries: not, at least, in the same incarnation. The heroic American ideal of agrarian conquest had proved its value in the era which was lapsing. But as the era lapsed into history so too did the ideal, along with its embodiment in the traditional American hero himself. In historical particulars that hero was passing swiftly into history, and even more swiftly into mythology. Essentially he had been a man of physical action sprung from instinctive moral impulses, and physical action, however derived, seemed an inappropriate sword to unsheath in the path of a blossoming technology, let alone in the still-to-be-opened path of a rampaging technology.

True, in limited respects such a hero would survive. But the survival would operate most significantly at the higher levels of political power, where a calculating man given to reason and an instinctive man-of-action could operate as one and the same and therefore as either, depending upon the requirements of particular confrontation. On down and closer to home the old hero would be more a new memory, his abilities inadequate and his disabilities disqualifying for assumption of a necessary new heroic role in an unavoidable new age which would carry the technological power to render human heroism obsolete. And heavy bets could be laid that the faces carved on Mount Rushmore would erode long before a corporate ideal of technological expansion would be universally accepted as an equally fulfilling substitute for the old hero's philosophical impetus.

There loomed, then, a void in the life of the country, and it fell upon the author to fill it. For who was better prepared to take on the slack in the nation's life-blood than the creative discoverer equally adept at employing his strength to reach backward or to reach forward—backward to preceding experience to resurrect previous events so as to define their relation to present acts, forward to uncharted drifts where the points of a better future could be signaled early by sifting present experience for definitions of both the blessings and the curses of a present age.

Thus, the bridge running from nineteenth-century America to twentieth-century America seemed to support what would be a further shift, in context perhaps the most vital shift of all—a transition not of heroic ideal into heroic ideal, but rather of actual hero into actual hero. If, then, the twentieth century would contain the technological power to displace human heroism as a viable human ambition, it would also and in contrast to this power contain the passage of old indigenous hero as a man of physical action to new indigenous hero as a man of written effort. To be sure, the shift would not be without its salient philosophical links. It would run, say, from David Crockett (who wrote books, in the contemporary American fashion, when not hunting and freedom-fighting) to, say, Ernest Hemingway (who hunted and freedom-fought, in the contemporary American fashion, when not writing books), such that the links themselves would never be without an inspirational continuity. But where the traditional American hero had received his sanction from the American author by way of the thrust of heroic ideal, now the modern American author stood not only within the shadow of a different ideal, but also—or alternatively—within a shadow cast by his own weight and constructed as offset to that ever-expanding shadow cast by the new ideal. Just as the author might choose to ally himself with technological change, he would be charged with deliberating the sanction of a modern ideal of more limited psychological attraction and of otherwise unlimited psychological reach.

Was this accelerating apocalyptic zone of interacting interest and impact understood by those who worked for many years during the first decade of the twentieth century to produce the Copyright Act of the United States, which finally emerged in 1909? No, the probabilities are too slim, the interests involved with writing and rewriting the federal copyright laws too many and too conflicting, the intellectual currents of necessity too soaked with the spirit of grace achieved through compromise. Yet there were distinguished members of the bar involved with the manipulation of that compromise, and it cannot be presumed that they took their responsibilities to the author, the public, and the law lightly. To be sure, the metaphysics of natural justice interested them not a whit further than instinct and ancestry might subtly allow. However, matters of honorable agreement between forces bound in common cause and in equal faith were something else; these came to the fore of conscience even if matters of cosmic insight were beyond the conceptions of most.

Thus, the moral and communal affirmation of ancient vintage, and now of American tradition, was not to wither in a new era of American life. Instead, it would become in the Copyright Act of 1909 a reaffirmation of utilitarian goal and ethical pledge. And if the author was now more valuable than ever before, with the attending societal goal more important than ever before, so then the duties of the public and the law to the author would be broader than ever before, with their attending pledges more sacred than ever before. For the community supporting this reaffirmation was larger now, and therefore the morality of the bargain emerged that much tighter, inseparable as it was from the betterment of a society which had become more intricate in its needs, and in its multiplicity of needs, more cut off from past senses of solution. Increases in the author's share of the bond would inhere in the legislation; references to the public's position would form the soul of the legislative history, and they would not be unfamiliar. The following is drawn from the "Report on the Bill Enacting the Copyright Act of 1909" (H.R. Rep. No. 2222, 60th Cong., 2d Sess. 7 (1909)):

> The enactment of copyright legislation by Congress under the terms of the Constitution is not based upon any natural right that the author has in his writings, for the Supreme Court has held that such rights as he has are purely statutory rights, but upon the ground that the welfare of the public will be served and progress of science and useful arts will be promoted by securing to authors for limited periods the exclusive rights to their writings. The Constitution does not establish copyrights, but provides that Congress shall have the power to grant such rights if it thinks best. Not primarily for the benefit of the author, but primarily for the benefit of the public, such rights are given. Not that any particular class of citizens, however worthy, may benefit, but because the policy is believed to be for the benefit of the great body of people, in that it will stimulate writing and invention to give some bonus to authors and inventors.

Of continued necessity, then, the twentieth-century American author would have at least as great a personal freedom as his literary and artistic forebears had had. But what now would be the width of the avenue by which his protection might proceed? In an earlier age, the traditional American hero—being a man of physical action—could ride out not only to conquer the frontier, but also to protect his newly claimed property by delivering justice where justice was due to those who would take his property from him. If the former course was an option inhering in the heroic ideal of the earlier era, election of this option often made the latter course a necessity during the same period. This was so because, in a substantially uncivilized environment, property rights conferred by law were one thing—the practical reach of the law in insuring protection

INTRODUCTION

of those rights was something else. So, quite rightly, the law of the frontier had manifest itself often enough as a natural law of self-help.

In a new age, a modern hero could carry on part of this tradition, not by riding out to conquer the frontier, certainly, but rather by writing out against new forces reared partly by the disappearance of the frontier itself. Yet still another effect of civilization was to eliminate the distance between legal right and legal enforcement, such that the twentieth-century American author could neither channel physical action nor written effort into *personally* insuring protection of his property. Where the nineteenth-century frontiersman could saddle Old Paint, charge Old Betsy, and then ride out to deliver an old-fashioned comeuppance to the thief who had stolen his land or his herd, twentieth-century law was not so set apart from its own enforcement centers that it would allow the twentieth-century author to avail himself of the same tradition when it came to running in a thief who had stolen *his* property. Just as self-help had been a workable legal ethic when the absence of civilization made chaos the only—and unacceptable—alternative, so self-help emerged as a chaotic legal alternative itself once civilization had rested the reach of the law within pervasive mechanisms of legislatively established law enforcement. So, then, the author would have great freedom conferred by great protection within the law to carry forward an American tradition of riding out. But when it came to *actual* protection of the author, the law would do the riding out and the running in for him.

Enter the criminal copyright law. The Copyright Act of the United States laid forth many civil remedies for copyright infringement and several formulas for calculating monetary damages in a variety of infringement situations, but for the first time in American copyright law these provisions were set within a blanket of protection which would allow thieves of creative property to be shrouded in the legal attire of the crook. On its face the law would speak for no-nonsense protection of the author's property rights, as it established the power of the federal justice system to place copyright pirates in jail. That American copyright law went so far so suddenly was a further effect of the new age—because the new age was to produce a new pirate.

This twentieth-century pirate was a product of the commercial flush of twentieth-century technology, technology being the force which gave the pirate his real power. Certainly, it was a greatly beneficial characteristic of technology that it produced new patterns of access to and use of creative property. But since technology could bear both good and evil, where it was not controlled technology afforded ready access to creative property which could be employed to further evil use. If, for instance, the author now had access to phonograph recording technology and motion picture technology, so did the pirate. And if the public now had access to the author's creative work as contained in any one of these technologies, so did the pirate. Though the manner in which the author used such technologies to disseminate his work would be legitimate, the fact that the pirate's use of such technologies to appropriate the author's work would be illegitimate would not alone bar the pirate from physical use of the same technologies. After all, prior control over the use of technologies in a free society was to be borne only in the most sensitive technological areas.

Thus, what the author originated and made available through such technologies, the pirate could easily appropriate through technological duplication. Even where the author confined the availability of his work to one technology, the pirate could appropriate the work as it existed in one technology and then make it available through another technology. Even if an author's work had been put in a form amenable to technological distribution but had not yet been made publicly available through any technology, the pirate could appropriate the work in its nest and then make it available through a suitable technology.

In the marketplace, the pirate might sell his stolen goods more cheaply than the author's work was available legitimately. Or the pirate might sell his stolen goods as expensively as the author's work would have been priced had it been made available legitimately. In either case, however, the pirate would bear only the costs of physical transfer and physical reproduction, together with his marketing cost. These would stand in contrast with a multiplicity of additional costs borne by the author and his investors in originating the work and in putting it in a form amenable to technological distribution.

In the same marketplace, the public would have access to the products of both author and pirate, if the public did not have access to the products of *only* the pirate. Whatever the case, however, the public would seldom be aware of the legal status of the available products. Where both legally delivered creative goods and illegally delivered creative goods were available and the public purchased pirated stock, all those including the author who were legally entitled to income from the sale of these creative goods would not receive the income generated, and that much fewer legally available creative goods could be sold. Where only illegally delivered creative goods were available, such that the public purchased nothing but pirated stock, all those legally entitled to the income generated again went unremunerated, and the economic value of the author's work fell precipitously, since the market for his legally deliverable creative goods was narrowed. In either case, the fact that illegally derived income from creative goods was being generated meant that tax revenues would be denied to the federal, state, and municipal governments—because it was characteristic of the pirate that he almost never paid taxes on his illegal income.

Thus, the pirate not only rode mighty in the commercial flush of twentieth-century technology, he rode low in that flush and was responsible for turning part of it into a major problem. By every moral and economic standard he was a parasite, and twice a parasite at that: he fed first by preying upon the author, and again by preying upon the public. By the same standards the pirate also emerged as one of the most interesting contradictions of the new age. While his decision to function in society as a parasite could only evolve from the loss of that nerve which allows a man to relate to society through honest labor, he could not live outside the law without courage, albeit misplaced. And while the pirate might show some of the best instincts of the entrepreneur, he would stamp himself a capitalist while shunning that real investment risk of entrepreneurship which makes capitalism an honorable economic pursuit.

However, the pirate could stomach whatever social stigmas he carried because his appetite was devoted primarily to those economic gains which are associated with creative enterprise, but which may be attached without benefit of either creative effort or creative investment. His implicit goal was to siphon to himself a substantial part of what society was prepared to give to the author as a return for whatever the author might be encouraged to give to society. The greatest evil of the pirate's operation lay lurking in this goal, because the author could not be made the object of economic theft without the public being made the eventual bearer of cultural loss. The essential danger of the pirate's societal function lay similarly rooted, because the pirate threatened nothing less than the disintegration of that delicately balanced atmosphere "in which authors and other creative artists can flourish." And as the twentieth century moved through time to reach not much beyond its half measure, this atmosphere came to be polluted with private larceny which went unpunished, public victimization which went unmended, and defiance of law which went unanswered.

Historically, the American process began when the twentieth-century American pirate became a noticeable force following the 1920s and the end of the "Jazz Age" in American culture. Early piratical efforts were directed against the music industry, and by any measure these efforts were small in scale, though certainly large in the industry-wide frustration they engendered. Jazz piracy remained an occupational disease among collectors of jazz recordings throughout the 1930s. But by the 1940s the more incorrigible of these collector-pirates were devising labels upon which to issue the stolen musical property, setting up shops to stock their illicit wares, circulating mail-order catalogs to tap the national collector trade, and making arrangements with regular wholesalers to achieve national retail distribution of their stolen goods.

Many of these pirate organizations were driven out of business when the legitimate record companies began to mount costly opposition to the record piracy fraternity in the early 1950s. At the same time, however, many other pirate organizations shifted from in-house setups to hit-and-run operations. And many new record piracy outfits moved into the hit-and-run piracy business, jumping from state to state in their efforts to keep one step ahead of the pursuing record companies. These pirates were not bothered by federal criminal authorities, nor could they have been. While the federal Copyright Act had made *most* copyright infringements for profit criminal, record piracy itself had been excepted from federal criminal copyright status.

Not so with motion picture piracy, which became prevalent in the 1960s when it was discovered that resorts, hotels, colleges, and film collectors provided a large and ready market for pirated prints of motion pictures. Thus the film pirate joined the record pirate in nefarious national enterprise. By the end of the 1960s their joint endeavors were costing the entertainment industry hundreds of millions of dollars each year. That translated into a problem agreeably out-of-hand. Moreover, American piracy had yet to play *its* hand through. In the 1970s, the soundtrack pirate appeared. Bearing features of both record piracy *and* film piracy, soundtrack piracy was far less economically important than either, but it also emerged as far more visible and defiant in its operation than either record piracy or film piracy.

By this time, record piracy had been made a federal crime and—in many states—a state crime. The federal law enforcement authorities could now move against record piracy, and they were preparing to move against film piracy as well. Still, a mighty rub was to lie in the facts that not until 1972 were record pirates brought before the bar of federal criminal justice, and that not until 1975 were federal criminal indictments filed and convictions obtained against film pirates. An equally sharp rub currently lies in the fact that, to date, not a single soundtrack pirate has even been indicted, though soundtrack piracy has always been more vulnerable to the applied reach of the criminal law than either record piracy or film piracy has ever been.

But the law, both in substantive reach and in aggressive action, was not the only actor in the play of piracy to change during the 1970s. Piracy itself also changed during this period, and it changed by becoming more corporate in its behavior. To be sure, in its lack of social responsibility and social respectability, piracy could not be described as corporate

INTRODUCTION xxxi

during this period—not yet. Rather, in its establishment of management/ employee/independent contractor setups, in its dependence on outside capital and in its use of inside capital, in its fascination with deceptively advertising its products as legal and culturally beneficial, in its arrangements with entrenched distribution facilities, in its calculation of distribution procedures yet untried, in its direction of large amounts of money into lobbying efforts to turn the criminal copyright law around, in its varying patterns of organized action and organized defense, in its acute intracompetitiveness, and in its desperate desire to proclaim its leaders as "creators," piracy turned corporate in behavior because its ambition was to be corporate in fact. Yet the corporate ideal aspired to by piracy was in fact an ideal as much on the dark side of technological advance in ambition as piracy itself had been on the dark side of technological advent in origin, such that the world of piracy became not a world of honorable or even defensible corporate affairs, but rather a polymorphic world characterized by heavy financing from organized crime, secret factories producing illegal sound recordings, public laboratories turning out illegal film prints, nocturnal telephone threats to the homes of investigative authorities, pulled-back jackets revealing hidden guns, quick-buck middlemen, shoddy tapes, unlistenable records, grainy films, deceptive packaging, mendacious advertising, clandestine strategy sessions sprouting robbery plans, lines of housewives working master duplicating machines, shifts of college student part-timers manning hydraulic presses, armed guards leading fierce dogs while guarding pirate plants, film piracy operations springing up in schools to feed the requirements of other schools, record piracy operations originating in storefronts to feed moms-and-pops, soundtrack piracy operations offering rewards for the delivery of master film music tracks, diversification into narcotics, pirate factories blown up in the night, jurisdictional wars, and by millions of illegal sound recordings and thousands of illegal film prints passing in interstate and foreign commerce each year.

But wait: the pirate was not to be without his defenders. No, indeed. In the midst of a dialectic underlying a balance between personal right and public good, and set against the entrenchment and expansion of that balance wrought by technological change, there would emerge defenses of the pirate often born of the technological age themselves. In these the pirate would take wing as musical and cinematic savant, as social benefactor spreading economic service in his wake, as no less than a cultural hero—a Robin Hood pirate stealing from the rich author and from his richer corporate investor to give to the poor public which itself had been victimized by the law. So the pirate was suddenly hailed in some quarters as a creature not of darkness but of light. And in the same quarters those who were prepared to fight the pirate were suddenly claimed to be figures not of good but of evil. The following is drawn from an editorial appearing in the May 1975 *RTS Music Gazette*, the monthly publication of a California organization which for a number of years has been not only a major but an outspoken consumer supplier of pirated and bootlegged soundtrack albums:

> The reissues [*sic* for pirate and bootleg soundtrack albums] at least provided an avenue by which soundtrack collectors could obtain some of the great film music that was not available to them—Marnie, From the Terrace, Love Is a Many-Splendored Thing, etc. There is also talk of including in the copyright infringement such items as the old radio shows and related nostalgia recordings. When a "witch-hunt" begins, our legislators are always quick to take it to the "nth" degree. Unfortunately, they are slow to move on any efforts on behalf of the average citizen, but jump when big business is concerned or when a topic is politically popular.

Excepting the ironically appropriate usage of the term "witch-hunt," which has a meaning in copyright discussion wholly different than the political meaning here intended, one could move swiftly to label this dictum perverse nonsense if not for the fact that there have been those, often in the academies, prepared to turn moral nonsense into amoral sense by lending intellectual support to the transformation. To be sure, this support has not been concerned with attacking the law as what Wilkie Collins called "the pre-engaged servant of the long purse." Rather, it has been directed against the twentieth-century extension, or even the twentieth-century existence, of a protectionist copyright law itself.

The traditional tactic of anticopyright theorists both quasi and magnus has been to attempt to identify the essence of copyright with certain repressive political measures which historically happened to precipitate the Statute of Anne in England. If the invention of the printing press during the fifteenth century presented problems for authors, it also coincided roughly with the Protestant Reformation and thereby engendered problems for the English Crown and the Catholic Church, both of which felt threatened by all writings opposing their power. In the sixteenth century an elaborate system of licensing acts was devised by England's autocratic government, whereby control over the press was concentrated in a political/religious/legal body known in infamy as the Star Chamber. The Star Chamber thereafter regulated all printing through a ban on unlicensed publishers, through monopoly grants to licensed publishers, and through censorship of their licensed publications. This system operated on behalf of what was claimed to be the public good, by keeping what were claimed to be seditious or heretical works out of the public reach. This system also deteriorated roughly in pace with the disintegration of political autocracy and the Church's influence in England, such that the enactment of the Statute of Anne in 1710 bespoke Parliament's observation that the old system was contrary to a policy of democratic reform, and moreover, that it had not worked even in a spirit of autocratic repression.

Though there are some similarities between the licensing system and a modern system of copyright—as where monopoly grants and notions of public good come into play—in important respects there are none. Copyright affords protection to the author, whereas the ancient licensing acts did no such thing. Copyright exerts no political control over the press, whereas the *heart* of licensing was political control over the press. Copyright is morally grounded in principles of human freedom and human optimism, whereas Star Chamber licensing was morally mired in tenets of human repression and human pessimism.

Nevertheless, some who have been interested in attacking twentieth-century copyright as repression incarnate have been equally fuzzy-headed enough to argue that modern copyright—in present reach, on future target, and at moral center—is exactly what ancient "copyright" was during the century and a half preceding the Statute of Anne. The argument continues to identify the Statute of Anne itself, and the Copyright Clause of the American Constitution thereafter, as nothing more than the twin ties that bind. This argument, while always entertaining, is being less and less intellectually tolerated today, and contemporary anticopyright theorists of intellectual stature do not make it. One reason is that the real weight in anticopyright argument of contemporary vintage has come to rest in a very different and much more powerful center.

It should come as no surprise at this point to find that this anticopyright center is not without substantial technological underpinning. Certainly, the web which surrounds the center has been spun creatively, largely by two very talented gentlemen from Harvard, Professors Ben Kaplan and Stephen Breyer. Still, the mark of the new technologist upon new anticopyright thesis is pervasive and unmistakable.

Kaplan's book, *An Unhurried View of Copyright* (Columbia University Press 1966, 1967), preceded by several years Breyer's massive law review paper, "The Uneasy Case for Copyright" (84 Harv. L. Rev. 281, 1970). While Kaplan, in his book, is indeed unhurried and even literate about what he has to say, Breyer, in his paper, is swift to bypass literary aspiration and eager to adapt the tools of the laboratory researcher and the computer programmer for devise of a case for copyright which is so uneasy that it reads like a final solution for copyright conceived in the locks of a mechanical Faustian exchange. Both writers direct their attention to societal efforts which may be made on behalf of the average citizen and with respect to the property rights of the author. The problem with their analyses is the same problem always inherent in anticopyright theory, for the only real moral value either writer acknowledges in his confrontation with copyright is expediency—and expediency is a technological value to be weighed morally, not a moral value to be institutionalized legally.

Kaplan's pet is plagiarism (which he equates effectually, for some undefined social ends, with piracy), while Breyer's favorite is piracy unadorned. Kaplan's argument on behalf of plagiarism lies in a call for increased public use of the author's creative work, the salve being that plagiaristic use is not *really* harmful to the author, and that it results in a broadening of the cultural base—and never mind *how* that expansion is derived. Breyer's argument on behalf of piracy arises by way of homage not to the prince of use but to the god of access; his justification is that no authors are entitled to protection anyway, that most modern authors do not create works for any purpose but access anyway, and that those authors who do create works for additional purpose and who would be harmed by piracy can make alternate contractual arrangements—with consumers, with government—to insure fair remuneration and thereby to mitigate economic damage. Neither Kaplan nor Breyer, mind you, is presenting a case for civil or criminal disobedience of copyright law. They are attacking the civil and criminal directions taken by copyright law in stifling plagiarism and piracy.

However, what is most interesting in their works is not so much an anticopyright concern with the role of the author in creative affairs, but rather an anticopyright concern with the role of the government in creative affairs. Breyer explores the possibility of doing away with copyright protection altogether and replacing it with a system of government subsidies to maintain authors' revenues. He admits that he has found no variation of the government subsidy approach which is both economically feasible and administratively practical. But he denies that selective publication or censorship of what is published presents the kinds of threats that would foreclose the idea itself. Kaplan, vastly more concerned with the danger of the thing than Breyer, doesn't like to see copyright law take itself too seriously, nonetheless. Quite seriously himself, however, he takes his thesis into what he acknowledges are Orwellian regions; there he offers the idea that "public utility" type copyright law or direct government ownership and control may be distilled of their dangers *if* "wise public regulation" *and* "humane development of the 'moral rights' of authors to prevent abuses in the exploitation of their creations" develop side by side in the brave new world of the future—and never mind the logic.

But what kind of cultural world will that be? No one has the answer, but Kaplan—always informed, ever brave, and eminently readable—has an opinion. It is offered following the introduction to the last of the three lectures which make up *An Unhurried View of Copyright*:

> The cult of originality, mentioned in the first lecture as having reinforced ideas of individual ownership of artistic productions, continues strongly into the present, although the forces that sustain it have undergone much change. Are there influences at work that will in time abate feelings of proprietorship and thus modify conceptions of copyright, especially those bearing on plagiarism? Probably so.
>
> Much intellectual work including the distinctively imaginative is now being done by teams, a practice apt to continue and grow. The French have a name for it—*travaux d'équipe*. Such collaboration, I fancy, may diffuse emotions of original discovery and exclusive ownership. I suggest, further, that the introduction of machines into the very creative process— computer-made music and poetry are crude examples of this development—will affect attitudes throughout copyright, besides raising difficult questions about copyrightability and infringement of the particular works. With mutations of machines, already imaginable, that foreshadow symbiotic relationships with the human brain, ideas of individuality and personality in relation to intellectual accomplishment may themselves be shaken.

I cite this projection here not to claim that Professor Kaplan is wrong (I think he is right about the identified influences and *their* potential impact), nor to imply that he looks forward to such a creative future with glee (I think his observations, in this respect, are neutrally drawn). Rather, I believe that the mechanistic airs of *a* creative future stirred by Kaplan's present projection allow an essential point to be better made, to wit: that it is one thing to allow the legal protection that we accord to creative property in the present to determine the creative future, and quite another thing entirely to allow a calculated view of the creative future to determine the legal protection that we accord to creative property in the present.

As I see it, the question which confronts us now is not whether a technologized creative future—technologized from delivery system back to deliverer and thereby sacked of an opportunity for moral exchange, personality, individual intellectual confrontation, emotionality, blood-run achievement, and everything else that makes creation a solitary human opportunity and a heroic human possibility—will come to be. The real question for us now is whether that is what we want. Because if we do want that, the easiest way to insure such a fate is to erode present copyright protection to such an extent that the only authors who will be able to operate without contempt for the law of creative property, or without disdain for a society which sanctions such an erosion, will indeed be subsidized team creators, laboratory creators, R&D creators, computer creators, and all other manner of machine creators—creators vastly more proficient than the individual author in stores of knowledge, calculation, abstract accuracy, and time requirements, but creators also vastly more deficient than the individual author in heart, passion, guts, and that precious wallop of unfettered individual imagination which allows beauty to be born apart from the machine and to be perceived through the conception of a single, fragile, human vision.

As with all futures, there is a choice in the matter, and I think it has come to rest in the present era. What we do with our law protecting creative property, and what that law itself does with those who steal creative property and defy the law to take action, affects not just the creative atmosphere and the nature of creative work which are a part of the present, but also the creative atmosphere and the nature of creative work which belong to the future. What moral agreements we have made in the past as a community living under law have proved valuable. If we now change those agreements into fundamentally different social arrangements, or if we now let those agreements stand or even if we reinforce them without giving them actual effect in the crunch, then it must be because the most serious and the most ancestral of our values have changed, because we have become or are prepared to live as a society set morally apart from the principles, the hopes, the daring, and the hard-won achievements which brought us into existence as a society in the first place.

In the end, a society's culture is nothing more than a reflection, born largely of creative endeavor, of that society's most prominent values. In every field of creative work, the kinds of authors and the natures of their works which we have today, and which we have had in the past, speak for the values that we have derived and retained up to the present moment. The kinds of authors and the natures of their works which manifest themselves from the present era on can only be determined by the values that we now retain, discard, or develop anew.

The present danger, then, is not that our authors and their corporate investors are stealing or will steal from the public by denying the public a control over their creative property. It is, instead, that the public itself might sanction our present pirates and their pseudo-corporate organizations in stealing from our authors and their corporate investors, assertedly in the agreeable name of public benefit, but actually in the acultural cause of amoral efficiency today, amoral deficiency tomorrow.

As will be seen, such a consumptive consumer direction is already rearing its head where the law has buried its own. It is in this evolution that the greatest and deadliest power of the pirate lies. For if the pirate is an evil force conceived in the blackest reaches of twentieth-century technology, it is finally because the pirate is the one product of technology capable of carrying technology's most frightening social potential into pervasive display. He feeds on that nourishment which belongs properly to the author, and through the author to the public. If he is allowed to take his fill, there will still be authors, and there will still be a public. But the public will run with little passion and less nerve, because its authors will run on oil, electricity, cardboard programs, and at the whim of government subvention.

The atmosphere in which creativity can flourish is fragile. It does not originate without sacrifice, and it cannot exist for very long without a balance of faith between author and public, or without a legal force which makes the balance genuine. Indeed, in its fragility, such a creative atmosphere is much like the physical atmosphere in which all persons live: pollute it too much, and it begins to fall apart. Squarely put, those who pollute this atmosphere by stealing creative property for private profit belong in jail, together with those who aid or abet such activity by "fencing" the stolen creative property to its consumers. This is more than a philosophical case which I happen to find based in private perceptions of moral right and communal faith. It is what American copyright law has established as a measure of responsibility to be borne by those who devote their labor to breaking copyright laws—laws which exist to protect the fruit of the labor of citizens, including authors, who live by those rules established for the benefit of us all.

In important respects, the process by which a polluted creative atmosphere is decontaminated is now underway. A federal criminal movement against the nation's record pirates was long in developing, but it is now an essential feature of the national war on crime. A federal criminal attack against the nation's film pirates was even slower to develop, but this too has become an important part of the drive to eradicate piracy. The natural third of these legal steps—a federal criminal response to the nation's soundtrack pirates—has yet to be taken. To be sure, the soundtrack pirate may not be the last of the cultural leeches to mobilize against the law. At present, however, the law bears the responsibility of insuring that this latest of the cultural leeches is set next in line for elimination.

How the law may achieve this third in a series of antipiracy movements, how every conceivable obstacle may be swept aside in bringing the nation's soundtrack pirates and their marketing associates to the bay of justice, and just how the soundtrack piracy network operates in this country, are questions of American piracy thus far unattended by the federal criminal justice system. These, then, are the questions I have attempted to answer in the balance of this book. Consider it a small act of writing out, meant to stir large acts of riding out, necessary acts of running in, and final acts of institutional faith in a societal bargain to which I subscribe.

The Great Motion Picture Soundtrack Robbery

The status of the motion picture soundtrack within copyright law, not yet judicially settled, has lately emerged more indistinct than ever it was before the current commercial fascination with vintage film music tracks and film dialog tracks took substantial root. Until recent writings on the subject began to sprout suggestions or insistences that the king has no clothes, motion picture attorneys had long thought the film soundtrack to be fully protected under the grant of motion picture copyright. With genuine assault upon that fairly orthodox assumption now under way, the protectionist assumption can hardly be called orthodox at the present time. Altogether, the greatest mischief has been made of the matter, such that the matter itself has become a multi-leveled mess. Not surprisingly, motion picture attorneys, motion picture makers, and law enforcement authorities are very confused and/or very frightened, for the dimensions of the mischief-making are unprecedented, as to both their interrelationship and the necessity for their dual resolution.

There is first that branch of mischief wherein legal commentary has plunged dangerously into an intellectual affair with fallacy. One commentator has insisted that "the copyright statute is inapplicable to motion picture sound tracks" and "[n]o amount of mental or semantic effort will accommodate sound tracks to the present copyright law."[1] Another commentator, somewhat more charitably, rationalizes an accommodation of that law to the film dialog tracks while positing a theory which, if sustained, would force the fall of thousands of film music

---

© 1975 Ken Sutak
* Mr. Sutak received a J.D. - M.B.A. at New York University in 1974. He is a member of the New York Bar.
[1] Brylawski, *Copyrightability of Motion Picture Sound Tracks*, 18 BULL. CR. SOC. 357, 370 (1971). [hereafter, Brylawski.]
[2] Yuzek, *Publication and Protection: In Qualified Support of the Copyright Office Approach to Motion Picture Soundtracks*, 22 BULL. CR. SOC. 19 (1974). [hereafter, Yuzek.]

tracks into the public domain.[2] The anti-protectionist attack has been directed against the embrace by Professor Nimmer, the United States Congress, the Copyright Office, and the motion picture industry, of the theory that "the express statutory recognition of copyright protection for motion pictures must be deemed to include the vital element of sound as contained therein . . . ."[3] Reasonably proper treatises and relevant cases have been culled and confronted in arriving at the anti-protectionist conclusions, to be sure. Yet settled motion picture history has been rewritten, orthodox motion picture theory has been disregarded, general motion picture industry practice has been misread and misrepresented, long established motion picture making techniques have been confronted with ignorance or not confronted at all, and the scan of the legislative histories has been as halting as the reading of relevant case law has been superficial. These lapses are serious, and they color the deviating conclusions to the point of unacceptability.

There is next that branch of mischief wherein anti-protectionist theory has been carried to the live and logical end of the great danger it presents. The world of record piracy needs no introduction here; the intricacies of that parasitic network have been well explored elsewhere and are generally understood by those who care.[4] What is not so well known, however, is that the most brazen element of the national pirate fraternity has in recent years been energetically devoted to appropriating and marketing—with burgeoning financial success—precisely what anti-protectionist theory would allow to be taken legally: the music tracks and/or the dialog tracks of most motion pictures produced during the era of sound-on-film. The current confusion in legal theory as to the protection accorded motion picture soundtracks in copyright law has not gone unnoticed by the pirates. Domestic soundtrack piracy—well organized, large scale, still growing rapidly, yet unresisted by force of law, and operating with such promotions as "[t]he legal staff of the manufacturer stated that this recording does not violate U.S. copyright requirements"[5]—is, in fact, virtually the only species of record piracy in which record pirates, record bootleggers, and record counterfeiters expect to and do operate openly, both on a national level and in accord with distribution methodologies and financing arrangements so unique as to be elsewhere unknown.

---

[3] 1 M. NIMMER, NIMMER ON COPYRIGHT 111-12 (rev. ed. 1974). [hereafter, NIMMER]

[4] *See* Yarnell, *Recording Piracy Is Everybody's Burden: An Examination of its Causes, Effects, and Remedies,* 20 BULL. CR. SOC. 234 (1973).

[5] *See* note 221 *infra.*

With this strange intertwining of promulgated theoretical sanction and proliferating physical expropriation now imbedded in our legal concern and in our economic concern with motion picture property, a collision course appears to have been charted which may well lead to the first frontal judicial consideration of the long dormant soundtrack copyrightability issue. The dominant purpose of this analysis is to unravel the legal confusion stirred and to undo the theoretical damage wrought. For it must be fact rather than fallacy, logic as opposed to antilogy, and a structurally harmonious perception of the relevant copyright law which neither breeds new confusions nor raises old problems into new prominence, that predicate whatever authoritative construction lies ahead regarding the precise reach of motion picture copyright.

Moreover, if the theoretical license of concern may be stripped of its analytical moorings, then the parameters and pitfalls of the collision course itself must be traced, analyzed, and fully understood. That charge rises if soundtrack piracy is to be effectively eradicated; thus, that charge rises as an ancillary purpose of this analysis. For if the motion picture soundtrack may be identified as protected by motion picture copyright, then, the implications of *Goldstein v. California*[6] notwithstanding, the illicit soundtrack record product may be identified as occupying a unique position in the relationship of federal copyright law to state anti-piracy laws, such that the *same* piratical product or activity often may be brought simultaneously within the jurisdictional purviews of *both* the federal and the state criminal authorities.

It is, altogether, a copyright problem which can be settled only when the legal analyst borrows from the tools of the film historian, the musicologist, the psychologist, and the journalist, while employing more familiar insights in burrowing to the crux of copyrightability itself. The solution to the soundtrack problem lies necessarily within such a maze, and a journey through such a maze might best begin by identifying both the range of the problem and those attending technical and legal considerations that shape its solution.

I. THE SOUNDTRACK COPYRIGHTABILITY CONFLICT

(A) The Motion Picture Soundtrack: Technical Identity and Legal Vulnerability

To begin with, two things must be recognized, for they bear importantly on subsequent analysis.

---

[6] 412 U.S. 546 (1973).

1. First, the motion picture soundtrack as a physical entity is, technically, a piece of film which contains the sound portion of a motion picture. As such, it is one half of any motion picture produced during the sound-on-film era; the second half consists of another piece of film which contains the photographic portion of a motion picture. The motion picture property, then, is a visually appreciable unity comprised of two integrated pieces of film. If the photographic piece of film (the visual track) and the sound piece of film (the soundtrack) are separated, the former still lends itself to some visual appreciation, but the latter does not.

The isolated soundtrack actually consists of a number of soundtracks which have individual identities. The unified soundtrack is born in the process known as dubbing. In dubbing, all of the sound elements to be employed in the film, which may be spread over as many as several dozen individual soundtracks, are combined into a single soundtrack by recording all of the individual soundtracks concurrently. For instance, in any given motion picture, the final soundtrack will generally have been produced by combining several dialog tracks, from three to thirty music tracks, and from ten to twenty sound effects tracks.[7]

In the discussion which follows, usage of the term "soundtrack" refers to the final soundtrack produced by the synthesis of all individual soundtracks. When the dialog tracks, the music tracks, or the sound effects tracks are intended to be considered separately, they are noted specifically. It is also important to note that the music tracks contain the underlying film music of a motion picture, while the dialog tracks contain the underlying dramatic work of a motion picture.

2. Second, identification of the legal vulnerability of the motion picture soundtrack is necessary, if only to fully understand the consequences of soundtrack uncopyrightability. It is quite incorrect to suggest, as at least one anti-protectionist commentator has done,[8] that there has ever been anything like an "industry practice" by which motion picture companies have sought to protect the film music heard on their music tracks independently or in lieu of whatever protection is afforded by motion picture copyright. It is more correctly the case that where motion picture companies have perceived some commercial value in musical themes, songs, or other musical compositions contained within their music tracks, then, and only then, have these isolated musical compositions been treated

---

[7] Gold, *Ernest Gold on the Mechanics of Scoring*, in T. THOMAS, MUSIC FOR THE MOVIES 26, 29 (1973).
[8] Yuzek, *supra* note 2, at 26.

apart from the motion picture copyright, by lending them separate notice and registration.[9]

For the vast majority of motion pictures made in this country since the era of sound-on-film began, such commercial perception has not occurred, and separate registration has been the exception, not the rule. Almost all of the original film scores composed during the 1930s and 1940s, as well as most of those composed during the 1950s and 1960s, were deemed inherently non-commercial save for their theatrical function in movie theaters. Hence, tens of thousands of hours of motion picture music are protected, if at all, only by grant of motion picture copyright.[10]

Similarly, motion picture screenplays were and are very rarely copyrighted as dramatic compositions apart from the protection afforded by grant of motion picture copyright.[11] Thus, the story-telling elements or dramatic works which inhere in the dialog tracks of thousands of motion pictures are protected, if at all, only by grant of motion picture copyright.[12]

(B) The Protectionist Claim

Since there is no judicial decision holding the motion picture soundtrack protected by motion picture copyright, protectionist theorists have extrapolated their views from a number of judicial and legislative developments which, combined, lend weight to an assertion of soundtrack

---

[9] So long as the Copyright Office maintained a neutral position on the copyright status of film soundtracks (*see* text accompanying notes 39-44 *infra*), separate treatment of film music could be granted via section 12 registration as unpublished musical works, either before or after release of the motion picture. Section 5(e) registration was alternatively permissible once film music was separately published.

[10] *See* Bernstein, *Collection News*, FILMMUSIC NOTEBOOK, Autumn, 1974, at 3, 4. Note that "most of the materials, that is, scores and parts (for the musicians) of motion pictures made before the 1950's, have either been destroyed, lost, or stored in such a way that it is impractical to attempt to retrieve them."*Id.* Hence, not only have most film scores not been separately registered in printed form, most of them no longer exist in printed form.

[11] Under a Copyright Office position of neutrality, the film screenplay manuscript, rather than its embodiment on film, could be registered in section 5(d) as a dramatic composition, or in section 12 as an unpublished dramatic composition. The registration could be made in section 5(c) as an address prepared for oral delivery if the manuscript contained only the words spoken on the film soundtrack. *See* A. LATMAN, HOWELL'S COPYRIGHT LAW 37 (rev. ed. 1962). [hereafter, LATMAN.]

[12] NIMMER, *supra* note 3, at 114.

copyrightability. Perhaps the best summary of the protectionist theory to be found in the treatises is Professor Nimmer's presentation:

> It would seem more realistic to recognize that "talkies are but a species of the genus motion pictures" and that indeed "talkies" or sound motion pictures have become virtually the only form of motion pictures now being produced. Therefore, the express statutory recognition of copyright protection for motion pictures must be deemed to include the vital element of sound as contained therein, and that to that extent Congress has modified the then extant general principle of denying copyright to sound recordings.[13]

This statement is not devoid of difficulties, as the motion picture classifications were added to the federal copyright law by the Townsend Amendment[14] in 1912, a time substantially predating the technological attachment of film soundtrack to film visual track. Nimmer argues that the congressional modification alluded to above flows from the reasonable meaning of the statutory language rather than from any analysis of legislative intent.[15] The assumed irrelevance of the latter, as well as an isolation in time of the sound-on-film era without regard to the possible relevance of historical precedents, has been characteristic of the protectionist theory.

The protectionists instead support a "reasonable meaning" argument by drawing arrows from a legal quiver of a wholly different sort—the doctrine known as "species of the genus". According to this doctrine, a later-appearing "species" is sought to be protected in a federal statutory sense by reach of the antecedent copyright recognition extended to an invisibly pregnant "genus". The "species of the genus" doctrine first emerged judicially in a motion picture soundtrack setting in *L.C. Page v. Fox Film Corp.*,[16] and then only in dictum:

> The development of mechanism making it possible to accompany the screen picture with the sound of spoken words was but an improvement in the motion picture art. As the plaintiff well says, "talkies" are but a species of the genus motion pictures; they are employed by the same theaters, enjoyed by the same audiences, and nothing more than a forward step in the same art. Essentially the form and area of exploitation were the same. The mere fact

---

[13] *Id.* at 111-12.
[14] Act of Aug. 24, 1912, 37 Stat. 488.
[15] NIMMER, *supra* note 3, at 112 n. 466.
[16] 83 F.2d 196 (2d Cir. 1936).

that the species "talkies" may have been unknown and not within the contemplation of the parties in their description of the generic "moving pictures" does not prevent the latter from comprehending the former.[17]

Despite the *Page* court's application of the "species of the genus" doctrine in dictum, this application has been cited with approval in one other case,[18] and anti-protectionist theorists have been unable to refute its logical relevance to the issue of soundtrack copyrightability.[19] The *Page* court spoke while construing the assignment of "exclusive motion picture rights." As one commentator has accurately noted, the issue of soundtrack copyrightability was not involved in the case and was probably removed from the court's thinking.[20] That hardly settles the matter, however, and even another anti-protectionist commentator concedes the transposition to and sustenance within a federal copyrightability setting of the "species of the genus" doctrine.[21] Yet the matter still remains alive, its heart carried in the question of *what to do* with the doctrine when approaching copyrightability analysis.

Three major developments occurred after the *Page* decision to buttress both the ranks of the protectionists and the conceptual support of their argument. None of these was judicial in setting, and all were logically derived.

1. The first development arose out of the legislative proposals made in 1952 to amend the copyright law so that the United States could participate in and comply with the provisions of the Universal Copyright Convention. Article I of the Convention states the protectionist philosophy of the Convention in terms of "cinematographic works" where motion pictures are concerned.[22] During the hearings on the amendments before the Senate Subcommittees on Foreign Relations and the Judiciary, several motion picture companies objected "that the motion picture industry would suffer serious prejudice from acceptance of the

---

[17] *Id.* at 199.
[18] Jerome v. Twentieth Century Fox-Film Corp., 67 F. Supp. 736, 742 (S.D.N.Y. 1946), *aff'd*, 165 F.2d 784 (2d Cir. 1948).
[19] This inability arises because the *Page* court, in construing the words of a contract, analogized to the statutory construction case of Kalem Co. v. Harper Bros., 222 U.S. 55 (1911), where the "species of the genus" doctrine was applied in a motion picture context. *See* text accompanying notes 126-28 *infra*.
[20] Brylawski, *supra* note 1, at 358.
[21] Yuzek, *supra* note 2, at 32.
[22] Article I, Universal Copyright Convention.

convention by the United States."[23] One specific objection made was "that the convention does not protect acoustic works such as the soundtracks of motion pictures."[24]

As the Senate Judiciary Committee report made clear,[25] other testimony given during the hearings, together with statements received thereafter from spokesmen for other motion picture companies, did not support the apprehensive claims.[26] Nevertheless, the fears of five motion picture companies were not allayed until a communication[27] from the Register of Copyrights to the chairman of the Senate Judiciary Committee was made available to attorneys representing the objecting companies. This communication relayed the following information.

The precise problem of soundtrack protection by means of the protection accorded "cinematographic works" by the Convention had been submitted in May, 1954, to the interim Inter-Governmental Copyright Committee,[28] convened pursuant to a resolution adopted by the Conference at Geneva, at a meeting of the interim committee held in Paris.[29] It had been the unanimous finding of the interim committee that:

---

[23] S. Rep. No. 1936, 83d Cong., 2d Sess. 10 (1954).
[24] *Id.*
[25] *Id.*
[26] Samuel W. Tannenbaum, representing the Copyright Association of America, appeared before the Subcommittees and expressed the opinion that "a motion picture film including the sound track either separately or as a whole, whether it be deemed a published or unpublished work, has protection under the Convention." Tannenbaum, *The Principle of 'National Treatment' and Works Protected,* in UNIVERSAL COPYRIGHT CONVENTION ANALYZED 13, 18 (T. Kupferman & M. Foner, eds., 1955). [hereafter, Tannenbaum.] *See Hearings on S. 2559 Before the Subcommittees on Foreign Relations and the Judiciary of the Senate,* 83d Cong., 2d Sess. 64 (1954). [hereafter *1954 Hearings*]. The same view was expressed in a report prepared by the American Bar Association which was "overwhelmingly approved by the patent, trade-mark, and copyright law section of the American Bar Association at its annual meeting in Boston during August 1953." S. Rep. No. 1936, 83d Cong., 2d Sess. 11 (1954). *See* ABA, REPORT OF THE COMMITTEE ON INTERNATIONAL COPYRIGHTS, in *1954 Hearings* 193, 201-02. Other spokesmen, appearing as counsel for independent motion picture companies, expressed similar views, *e.g.,* that "the sound track which is a part of a motion picture and which is presently protected will not be thrown into the public domain by any provision or application of the UCC." Statement of Adolph Schimel in Support of Executive M, and S. 2559, in *1954 Hearings* 188, 190.
[27] Letter from Arthur Fisher to Senator Alexander Wiley, June 8, 1954, in *1954 Hearings, supra* note 26, at 206.
[28] The Committee was comprised of five foreign delegates and Arthur Fisher, the United States Register of Copyrights. Tannenbaum, *supra* note 26, at 17.
[29] S. Rep. No. 1936, 83d Cong., 2d Sess. 10-11 (1954).

> Cinematographic works are provided for in [Article I] as forming a unified whole. In the case of a sound film (and these films were practically the only ones to be shown in cinemas at the time the Universal Convention was signed, 6 September 1952) the cinematographic work as such covers not only the part thereof comprising images but also sound.[30]

This finding of the interim committee was not offered as an official interpretation of the Convention's substantive treatment of motion pictures, but rather as the response of "individuals experienced in copyright and participants in the development of the Universal Copyright Convention."[31] Still, the opinion carried great weight with the Senate Judiciary Committee and the motion picture companies. The Committee, noting the express repudiation of the contrary view by the American Bar Association,[32] stated: "The opinion makes it abundantly clear that nothing in the present convention will result in the loss of any protection for the integrated sound portion of a motion picture which it now enjoys."[33] Prior to the submission of the Committee's report, attorneys representing the concerned companies formally withdrew their objections in a letter also stating:

> Each of us and the copyright counsel of our respective corporations are of the considered opinion that the present United States copyright law protects the sound and other parts of a motion picture as a unified whole. We are informed that counsel for other American producers of sound motion pictures are of the same opinion.[34]

2. That the United States Congress agreed with this view as early as 1954 was amply demonstrated in 1971 when Congress passed the Sound

---

[30] Letter from Professor Henri Puget to Luther Evans, May 20, 1954, in S. Rep. No. 1936, 83d Cong., 2d Sess. 11 n.1 (1954).
[31] *Id.*
[32] ABA, REPORT OF THE COMMITTEE ON INTERNATIONAL COPYRIGHTS, in *1954 Hearings, supra* note 26, at 193.
[33] S. Rep. No. 1936, 83d Cong., 2d Sess. 11 (1954). Note that the Committee's statement can be read as saying that "no protection for the integrated sound portion of a motion picture will be lost because no protection is now enjoyed." However, even the intimation of that notion by the Committee would have caused an uproar in the motion picture industry, so there is little doubt that the Committee's view on soundtrack protection in the United States was positive.
[34] Letter from Austin Keough to Senator Alexander Wiley, June 8, 1954, in *1954 Hearings, supra* note 26, at 207, 208.

Recording Act,[35] which may be identified as the second non-judicial development partially based upon and altogether supportive of protectionist theory. The amendment excludes from its coverage "sounds accompanying a motion picture".[36] The report of the House Judiciary Committee discusses the derivation of such treatment as follows:

> In excluding "the sounds accompanying a motion picture" from the scope of this legislation the Committee does not intend to limit or otherwise alter the rights that exist currently in such works. The exclusion reflects the Committee's opinion that soundtracks or audio tracks are an integrated part of the "motion pictures" already accorded protection under subsections (l) and (m) of Section 1 of title 17, and that the reproduction of the sound accompanying a copyrighted motion picture is an infringement of copyright in the motion picture. This is true whatever the physical form of the reproduction, whether or not the reproduction also includes visual images, and whether the motion picture copyright owner had licensed use of the soundtrack on records.[37]

Thus, the Committee essentially reiterated what had earlier been postulated—that the statutory copyright accorded motion pictures must be reasonably deemed to embrace the later developed soundtrack, with the preceding congressional policy of denying copyright to sound recordings being seen as modified by the dual impact of technological circumstance and legal implication. The Committee did not, however, deal directly with either the film music underlying the film music tracks or the film dramatic work underlying the film dialog tracks. Nor had protectionist theorists much confronted these ancillary issues previously, except to assume implicitly, in accord with the statutory recognition that a copyright shall protect all of the copyrightable component parts of a work copyrighted,[38] that a motion picture copyright protecting the soundtrack would also protect the film music and the film dramatic work underlying the music tracks and the dialog tracks, respectively, from which the soundtrack itself had been constructed.

---

[35] Act of Oct. 15, 1971, 85 Stat. 391.
[36] The Sound Recording Act provides for the copyrightability of sound recordings, which are defined as "works that result from the fixation of a series of musical, spoken, or other sounds, but not including the sounds accompanying a motion picture." Act of Oct. 15, 1971, 85 Stat. 391, *amending* 17 U.S.C. §26.
[37] 117 Cong. Rec. 1566, 1570-71 (1971).
[38] 17 U.S.C. §3.

3. However, administrative attention to these issues and to the parent issue as well arrived swiftly once the Sound Recording Act became effective.[39] The amendment presented a number of sound recording registration problems for the Copyright Office. One of these was the question of what to do with recordings submitted for registration and identified as soundtrack albums.[40] The direction of the administrative inquiry elected was toward whether the sounds of the submitted article were originally fixed in a motion picture soundtrack and first published by distribution of the integrated motion picture.[41] Notwithstanding the divergence of decisions[42] as to whether or not the lease, exhibition, or release of a motion picture constitutes a publication of the motion picture, the procedural administrative inquiry necessitated by the Sound Recording Act with respect to registration of soundtrack albums also mandated the establishment of a symmetrical administrative policy with respect to registration of the underlying film music. The Copyright Office's position on the copyright status of motion picture soundtracks had formerly been neutral,[43] but the spur provided by the new procedural necessities made elimination of this neutrality a necessity itself. Whereas applications for unpublished copyright in musical compositions appearing on the soundtracks of distributed motion pictures had formerly been accepted by the Copyright Office, this policy was suddenly reversed, with the Copyright Office taking "an affirmative position that a sound motion picture is an

---

[39] The provisions for copyrightability of sound recordings in the Sound Recording Act took effect on Feb. 15, 1972.
[40] Keziah, *Registration Problems Encountered by the Copyright Office Under the Recent Sound Recording Amendment,* 20 BULL. CR. SOC. 3, 13 (1972).
[41] *Id.*
[42] The assumption has always been that commercially leased motion pictures are published, upon analogy to Jewelers' Mercantile Agency Ltd. v. Jewelers' Weekly Pub. Co., 155 N.Y. 241, 49 N.E. 872 (1898) (commercial leasing of books to subscribers constitutes publication). *See also:* Patterson v. Century Productions, Inc., 93 F.2d 489 (2d Cir. 1937), *cert. denied,* 303 U.S. 655 (1938) (limited, non-commercial exhibition of motion picture does not constitute publication); Blanc v. Lantz, 83 U.S.P.Q. 137 (Cal. Super. Ct. 1949) (musical laugh recorded on motion picture soundtrack and distributed via commercial leasing of motion picture is published, under state law defining publication, so as to divest common law rights). *Contra,* Brandon Films v. Arjay Enterprises, 33 Misc. 2d 794, 230 N.Y.S.2d 56 (1962) (general, commercial exhibition of motion pictures does not constitute publication). Note that the state statute involved in *Blanc* has since been repealed, and that the investiture of statutory rights via publication was not an issue in the case.
[43] Letter from Barbara Ringer to Dean Yuzek, April 29, 1974, in Yuzek, *supra* note 2, at 20 n.4.

entity, that copyright in a motion picture extends to all copyrightable component parts of the motion picture including those reproduced on soundtrack...."[44]

If the implication born of the wedding of protectionist theory with legislative sanction was not to remain administratively unattended for long, neither would an administrative effort to adjust a procedural inattentiveness of an earlier era, in view of its dislocating thrust,[45] escape criticism. One critic of the Copyright Office's action in this regard summarizes the theoretical parameters of that action as follows:

> ... the Copyright Office has adopted the position that motion picture release is not only divestive of common law protection of film music but is also capable of resulting in the investiture of statutory protection. The Copyright Office suggests that in order to protect their rights in film music, music publishers rely on the principle that the motion *picture* copyright includes, and therefore affords protection to, such film music.[46]

The statement would appear to be correct on its face as to the current Copyright Office position on soundtrack protection. It is to be noted, though, that any suggestion that the Copyright Office's proposed reliance is something *new* as to a general industry reliance *in fact* is decidedly specious. The vast preponderance of film music written during the sound-on-film era has been treated by motion picture companies exactly as the Copyright Office now insists that it be treated—as protected by motion picture copyright and nothing more.[47] The Copyright Office

---

[44] *Id.*
[45] Although most film music had never been separately registered, the film music which had been separately registered comprised enough of a publishing activity to generate confusion among publishers of film music when the Copyright Office changed its practices. *See* Yuzek, *supra* note 2, at 26.
[46] Yuzek, supra note 2, at 1-2. (emphasis in original).
[47] This insistence operates only once the motion picture is commercially released and thereby published. Copyrighting printed versions of the film screenplay or the film music as section 12 unpublished works is still possible. Such pre-copyrighting via section 12 is, in fact, the solution urged by anti-protectionist theorists to prevent what are claimed to be otherwise unprotected film materials inhering in the film soundtrack from falling into the public domain. Brylawski, *supra* note 1, at 368: Yuzek, *supra* note 2, at 42. Since section 12 pre-copyrighting of current film materials of this nature, and even a prospective judicial application of anti-protectionist theory with regard to post-release copyrighting of these film materials in the past, would do nothing to prevent the vast preponderance of all such materials from falling into the public domain if anti-protectionist theory is judicially adopted, the anti-protectionist "solution" emerges at best as icing without the cake.

action, then, actually does little more than administratively affirm the theoretical base of a general, industry-wide practice which was ingrained long before the *Page* court, the Congress, and finally the Copyright Office itself, embraced a protectionist posture. Whether the protectionist voices have been correct, of course, is another matter, and one which subsequent analysis shall penetrate.

A number of loose analytical ends do emerge from what has been offered here as a summary of the protectionist claim as yet enunciated and of what is largely its extra-judicial direct support. Generally, these may be best identified within the realm in which they have received their most searching attention—that of anti-protectionist thought. However, mention may be made here of one issue which need not be resurrected as a point of contention germane to the issue of soundtrack protection —publication of the motion picture itself. That issue has arisen because the procedural symmetry which inheres in the Copyright Office's twin policies toward registration of soundtrack album recordings and registration of film music underlying film music tracks has been derived by positing a substantive symmetry between motion picture publication and functional protection of the soundtrack and its underlying elements. That there is considerable authority in support of the Copyright Office's position on motion picture publication has been urged and amply demonstrated elsewhere[48] and even within the context of anti-protectionist argument.[49] Hence, the issue need not be directly confronted here, though certain of its legal underpinnings carry relevant import to the issue of protection and must be considered accordingly.[50]

More importantly, "the ability to sustain the Copyright Office position on protection of the soundtrack would render its approach to divestive publication consistent with the symmetrical theory of copyright publication and protection...."[51] This result, in the context of anti-protectionist argument, has been claimed to be "not mandated by law but equally satisfying nonetheless."[52] Since it is through the identification and untying of those "loose analytical ends" of the protectionist claim that the fabric of protectionist theory may be wholly undone or reinforced, it is to the thrust of anti-protectionist theory that we now look.

---

[48] NIMMER, *supra* note 3, at 216-17.
[49] Yuzek, *supra* note 2, at 22-24.
[50] Since the anti-protectionists link cases dealing with the publication of music via distribution of phonograph records with authorities supporting motion picture publication, they proceed to equate phonograph records with motion picture soundtracks. For a consideration of this attempted equation, *see* text accompanying notes 63-73 *infra*.
[51] Yuzek, *supra* note 2, at 30.
[52] *Id.*

(C) The Anti-Protectionist Attack

The promulgation of anti-protectionist theory has been as splintered as the derivation of protectionist rationale has been logically uniform. While protectionist voices have remained congruent as to conceptual push, anti-protectionist tracts manifest some disagreement even while assailing the protectionist reasoning. Nevertheless, whether the consequence of a particular attack be the toss into the public domain of part or of all of the motion picture soundtrack and its underlying elements, anti-protectionist theorists share a strategical kinship through which the body of protectionist theory is penetrated and dealt its intended death blows not at its ideological jugular, but at its ramificatory veins.

Here, at least, the issue of the direction of legislative intent, so indelicately sidestepped by Professor Nimmer and others in traveling to an embrace of "species of the genus", is fully hauled into prominence. The impact of the asserted inability to bind an original legislative intent to the "reasonable meaning" thesis is by no means claimed to be devastating. However, it is suggested to be detrimental:

> The Act of August 24, 1912 amended the copyright law to embrace for the first time copyright in motion pictures. Such motion pictures at that time, of course, were only silent motion picture productions and "talkies" were not even in contemplation.....
> Some sixteen years later when sound motion pictures were made, first by the addition of a recording disc and subsequently by means of a sound track affixed to the film itself, the question became real whether the sound track was a copyrightable component of the entire motion picture production.
> That a sound track is not a copyrightable component of a motion picture derives partly from the fact that sound tracks as adjuncts to motion pictures were not in existence or contemplation at the time of the 1912 Act and, hence, it could not have been the intention of Congress to have included sound tracks at that time.[53]

That protectionist voices have not quarreled with this historical summary has been noted; that this historical summary has been accepted as an axiom from which springs further penetration into the protectionist claim is also evident. Thus, a devoted attention has been paid to the level of legal thought to which the absence of an original legislative intent leads: the "species of the genus" doctrine. What the protectionists have gripped on an *a priori* basis at this level of legal reasoning, the anti-

---

[53] Brylawski, *supra* note 1, at 360.

protectionists have been sharply—and divergently—circumspect in qualifying.

Thus, while one commentator has called for the rejection of *any* application of the *Page* court's "species of the genus" rationale to a determination of the soundtrack copyrightability question,[54] another has directed inquiry to the logical relevance of that rationale to the same question.[55] The latter pursuit has led to mention of the fact that prior to the passage of the Townsend Amendment, the motion picture had been judicially recognized as a protectible species of the genus "photograph" in *Edison v. Lubin*.[56] The *Edison* court had characterized the process by which the motion picture before it[57] was made as an "advance in making photographs".[58] In applying a "species of the genus" approach, the *Edison* court then held the film copyrightable as a photograph under a congressional amendment of 1865 extending copyright protection to photographs. In the context of anti-protectionist thought, however, the *Edison* analogy has been deemed unsatisfactory as authority for the application of a "species of the genus" rationale to the problem of soundtrack copyrightability, because:

> In *Edison*, both the "species" motion picture and the "genus" photograph were visually appreciable. The problem of the motion picture soundtrack is complicated by the presence of a visually appreciable genus (the motion picture) and an "integrated" element (the soundtrack) that renders the species ("talkies") decidedly *aural* in nature, as well as visual. It is this aspect of the problem which mitigates against complete acceptance of Professor Nimmer's "integrated element" approach to ultimate protection of the material recorded on a motion picture soundtrack.[59]

This analysis is not without problems of its own. One of these problems is that the analysis apparently offers a purely physical symmetry between genus and species as dispositive of whatever reasonable legal construction is called for by application of the "species of the genus" doctrine. However, the *Edison* court saw its responsibilities to reason mandated as a function of the object of the specific copyright act in question; this in turn

---

[54] *Id.* at 362.
[55] Yuzek, *supra* note 2, at 31-32.
[56] 122 Fed. 240 (3d Cir. 1903).
[57] The motion picture before the *Edison* court was an unedited film loop. *See* text accompanying note 110 *infra*.
[58] 122 Fed. at 242.
[59] Yuzek, *supra* note 2, at 33 (emphasis in original).

was identified as a function of the object of the constitutional grant of power "to promote the progress of science and useful arts."[60] The analytical erosion of what might be called a "reasonableness" requisite—a requisite potentially imbedded in "species of the genus" doctrine itself—apparently has been sensed as insupportable even while being tendered, for the analysis has been qualified:

> Reference was made earlier to the difficulty of applying a "species of the genus" approach, when the integral element for which protection is sought is aural in nature. Perhaps it is fair, however, to fall back upon the reason of the thing. Since the picture track of a film alone is relatively unintelligible, it is not unreasonable to say that the nature of the whole, when the soundtrack is joined with the visual band, is indeed different than the nature of the individual parts of that whole. The soundtrack, however, may be comprised of both dialogue and music. There may in fact be a valid dividing line to be perceived here; on one side may fall material contributions to beneficial use. Such contributions may be copyrightable as validly proclaimed *integral* elements of the whole. On the other side may fall those contributions to the whole which merely enhance enjoyment. If uncopyrightable individually, such contributions would remain uncopyrightable even when joined with a copyrightable work. Under the above analysis, the justice of the result would lie in the fact that the element which merely enhances enjoyment—as opposed to that which materially contributes to beneficial use—neither has its nature modified by association with the whole nor causes the nature of the whole to be materially modified. The dialogue portion of the soundtrack may be viewed as a material contribution to the beneficial use of the motion picture, the film music as an enhancement of enjoyment. It is our contention, then, that it may be proper in certain circumstances to afford protection to an aural element of an otherwise visual whole, on the basis of an "integral" element or "species of the genus" approach.[61]

It is a matter of no small importance that the originator of this "material contribution/enhancement of enjoyment" theory considers the film dialog tracks the only part of the motion picture soundtrack which can "even reasonably be deemed an integral element of the film under a species of the genus or entity approach to sound motion pictures."[62] Be

---

[60] 122 Fed. at 242, *quoting* U.S. CONST. Art. I, §8, cl.8.
[61] Yuzek, *supra* note 2, at 35 (emphasis in original).
[62] *Id.* at 37.

that as it may, the attachment of a "reason of the thing" or a "reasonableness" approach to considerations of visual appreciability and intelligibility does confer a substantial and embryonic conceptual importance to the analysis: one which may operate legally as well as independently of any arbitrary aesthetic distinctions drawn as to motion picture intelligibility itself. The legal ramifications of this conceptual frame will be considered fully in subsequent analysis, but a number of points concerning the peculiar anti-protectionist theory wedged into this conceptual frame may be noted here.

First, the substantive analysis as to what is integral and what is not establishes motion picture aesthetics as a frontal matter of legal consideration in application of the "species of the genus" doctrine to the soundtrack copyrightability question. Second, this particular entry into the domain of aesthetic analysis has been made without regard to the responsibilities attending aesthetic analysis itself. That is to say, the film dialog tracks may be material to motion picture intelligibility, and the film music tracks may be immaterial to such intelligibility, but it is hardly sufficient merely to state that the former are and the latter are not and then to offer a legal theory grounded in aesthetic distinctions drawn *a priori*. Third, any aesthetic analysis that might be made regarding the anti-protectionist theory posited within the conceptual frame introduced must look for support independent of motion picture aesthetic theory itself. For the concept of the motion picture art which emerges from this anti-protectionist rationale entirely contradicts that which has operated in motion picture making and motion picture theory since the motion picture was invented—*i.e.*, the quite universally accepted aesthetic notion that the motion picture art is a mosaic art in which elements of all the arts are integrated and interrelated.

Notwithstanding the difficulties attending the anti-protectionist theory constructed within the conceptual frame introduced, the frame itself remains symmetrically formidable because visual appreciability and intelligibility considerations may be as much mandated by law as a "reasonableness" factor may be legal part and parcel of a "species of the genus" analysis applied in a copyrightability setting. Attention in this respect has been drawn to *White-Smith Music Publishing Co. v. Apollo Co.*,[63] a case which the protectionists prefer to consider "tacitly modified insofar as motion picture sound tracks are concerned by the subsequent amendment which expressly added motion pictures as copyrightable works,"[64] despite the preservation of its rule with respect to phonograph records

---

[63] 209 U.S. 1 (1908).
[64] NIMMER, *supra* note 3, at 442.2. *Accord,* LATMAN, *supra* note 11, at 148-49.

until passage of the Sound Recording Act. The protectionist preference imbues protectionist theory with at least an uncomfortably facile analytical quality. The anti-protectionists will have no part of the "tacit modification" argument, and they may be as correct as they have been uniform in their objections, albeit in unforeseen fashion.

The Court in *White-Smith* held that a perforated piano roll was not an infringing copy of the musical composition embodied in the roll, because the roll was not a written or printed record of the musical composition in intelligible notation. The Court's equation of copyrightability with protectibility was clear,[65] and if the relevance of "copy" reproduction to copyrightability is familiar, it is also well known that the twin requirements of visual appreciability and intelligibility provide the two-fold test by which a *White-Smith* copy may be established. Just what analytical relation exists between these twin requirements is not quite clear. It has been suggested that application of the intelligibility test is a procedural function of positive application of the visual appreciability test.[66] Yet *how* to apply an intelligibility test, and *against what* to apply the visual appreciability test or the intelligibility test, can in certain circumstances become controversial issues.

Hence, it has been argued that "[a]s to soundtrack protection through the motion picture copyright, intelligibility breakthroughs matter little if the initial hurdle of visual perception remains extant."[67] However, this argument has been introduced by first *divorcing* the soundtrack from the visual track of the motion picture and then directing consideration to the soundtrack in isolation. Since the isolated soundtrack is not visually appreciable as to its underlying elements, the argument then continues to identify the soundtrack as uncopyrightable because it cannot be a copy of its underlying elements, in accord with the rule of *White-Smith*. Support for this argument is claimed to rise from the Copyright Office's practice of refusing to register either a lone soundtrack or a soundtrack offered as the only new matter in a previously published or registered motion picture.[68]

---

[65] After defining "copy" and denying that the piano roll was a copy, the Court stated, at 209 U.S. 17:
> The statute has not provided for the protection of the intellectual conception apart from the thing produced... but has provided for the making and filing of a tangible thing, against the publication and duplication of which it is the purpose of the statute to protect the composer.

[66] Yuzek, *supra* note 2, at 34. Note that the intelligibility test went unapplied in *White-Smith* when the piano roll was deemed incapable of visual appeal.

[67] *Id. Accord,* Brylawski, *supra* note 1, at 361.

If this argument initially appears salient, it palls considerably when examined as to its logical ramifications. The most immediately apparent of these is that a symmetrical analysis applied to the isolated visual track of the motion picture may result in deeming the isolated visual track as theoretically uncopyrightable as the isolated soundtrack has been claimed to be. For if the visual track of the motion picture is unintelligible in isolation while the soundtrack of the motion picture is visually unappreciable in isolation, then the former must fail the *White-Smith* test as easily and as severely as the latter. If this consequence is to be deemed legal lunacy, then so must any anti-protectionist argument constructed by isolating half of a motion picture be deemed unacceptable.

However, the absurdity of chopping up the motion picture in this fashion in order to posit anti-protectionist argument becomes clear only if the motion picture visual track is indeed unintelligible in isolation and therefore fails the *White-Smith* test in fact. Quite obviously, the judicial meaning accorded the intelligibility maxim emerges as a paramount analytical consideration. That the intelligibility maxim is ideational in essence we know from *White-Smith* itself.[69] Just how consummately ideational it is—and just how much the legal concern with aesthetic analysis already advanced is mandated by application of the conceptual frame of "species of the genus" doctrine already introduced—will shortly be seen.

The tactic of directing attention to the isolated soundtrack, adopted in order to invoke the bludgeon of *White-Smith*, and however discreditable in view of the impact which the identical legal ax may have on the isolated visual track, does allow the anti-protectionists to flesh out their theory with analogies to the judicial and legislative treatment of phonograph

---

[68] Brylawski, *supra* note 1, at 362. *Accord,* Yuzek, *supra* note 2, at 32. Brylawski claims that the Copyright Office recognized *White-Smith* as authority for denying the copyrightability of motion picture soundtracks when it issued the following rules in the *Copyright Office Rules of Practice,* No. 2.14.1, Chapter 2, page 47 of the "Compendium of the Copyright Office Practices 1967" under the sub-heading "III. Sound Tracks":
    b. Registration is not made for a sound track alone, or for a sound track as the only new matter in a previously published or registered motion picture.
    Examples: (1) An old silent picture with a new sound track
                (2) A previously published foreign film with a dubbed sound track in English.

[69] In arriving at its definition of a copy of a musical composition as "a written or printed record of it in intelligible notation," the Court in *White-Smith* quoted with approval the definition given by Bailey, J., in West v. Francis, 5 Barn. & Ald. 743: "A copy is that which comes so near to the original as to give every person *seeing* it the *idea* created by the original." 209 U.S. at 17 (emphasis added).

records. In this regard there has been a concerted effort to equate the isolated soundtrack with the phonograph record. Indeed, once the soundtrack has been isolated, the effort seems a logical imperative of anti-protectionist thought, for the preservation of the rule of *White-Smith* with respect to phonograph records and the traditional inability to secure statutory protection for phonograph records do confer an aura of uncopyrightability on the isolated soundtrack *if* the equation can be made.

Thus, attention has been drawn to the equation made between the isolated soundtrack and the phonograph record by some courts for other purposes.[70] It has also been argued that the isolated motion picture soundtrack is really of the genus "mechanical recordings".[71] Even where the dialog tracks of the (integrated) soundtrack have been proffered as protectible, the music tracks have been claimed to be expendable because:

> There is a clear practical distinction between the dialogue and music portions of the soundtrack. The music portion of the soundtrack may have a useful life above and beyond that of the motion picture itself, and is capable of being exploited long after the picture is no longer useful. On the other hand, the market for the dialogue portion of the soundtrack normally exists only as long as, and in conjunction with, the exploitation of the film. Such industry realities as these increase the tenability of the analogy of film music to phonograph records.[72]

However, the only clear thing about the "clear practical distinction" urged is that it has nothing to do with matters of integration or intelligibility vis-à-vis the aesthetic functions performed by the dialog and the music in the copyrighted motion picture. Moreover, even if irrelevant to the dominant motifs of copyrightability analysis, the purported "industry realities" emerge as fallaciously asserted when we note such historical realities as the fact that fully fifteen years of sound-on-film production had passed before *even one* original film score of an American film was considered to have a "useful life of its own" and was commercially ex-

---

[70] Foreign & Domestic Music Corp. v. Licht, 196 F.2d 627 (2d Cir. 1952) (license to publicly perform songs does not carry the right to reproduce the songs on film soundtrack); Encore Music Publications, Inc. v. London Film Productions, Inc., 89 U.S.P.Q. 501 (S.D.N.Y. 1951) (reproduction of songs on film soundtrack without synchronization license infringes recording rights). In *Foreign & Domestic Music,* Judge Learned Hand noted that the soundtrack reproduction infringed the copyrights in the songs by falling within section 1(e)'s grant to the copyright owner of an exclusive right to make any arrangement or setting of a musical composition in any form of record. 196 F.2d at 629.
[71] Brylawski, *supra* note 1, at 363.
[72] Yuzek, *supra* note 2, at 24.

ploited apart from its functional purpose in movie theaters.[73] While this "useful life of its own" consideration has shifted appreciably in recent years, it is still the case that the vast preponderance of film music written during the half-century sound-on-film era has in no way been commercially exploited apart from its functional cinematic purpose.

In further asserting the validity of the soundtrack/phonograph record equation, attention has been drawn to Professor Nimmer's contention that the motion picture soundtrack, unlike the phonograph record, is not the type of mechanical reproduction to which the compulsory license provision of section 1(e)[74] applies.[75] Nimmer's argument has been attacked because:

---

[73] Wick, *The Birth of the Spellbound Concerto*, PRO MUSICA SANA, Spring, 1973, at 4. Note that even when such commercial exploitation arrived, it literally had to be forced upon the record companies: the movie producers financed it. In 1943, David O. Selznick spent $12,000 to produce 1,000 transcription discs of some of Max Steiner's music from "Since You Went Away" ('43); these were unavailable commercially but received wide radio play, thus publicizing the film. The following year, Selznick employee Ted Wick tried to convince the record companies to record some of Miklos Rozsa's music from "Spellbound" ('44), but was turned down everywhere. Wick notes: "Jim Conkling, then head of Capitol, turned me down flat, adding that "the record-buying public isn't at all interested in movie music." *Id.* In desperation, the Selznick corporation subsidized a commerical release of a *Spellbound* recording, which became one of the most popular disc successes of the year. In response, record companies began issuing selected film music suites and soundtrack albums in 1945. However, such recordings remained few and far between until the mid-1950s, when at least a dozen or more soundtrack albums began to appear regularly each year—drawn from the several hundred original film scores recorded for motion picture soundtracks each year.

[74] 17 U.S.C. §(e) reads in appropriate part:
And as a condition of extending the copyright control to such mechanical reproductions, that whenever the owner of a musical copyright has used or permitted or knowingly acquiesced in the use of the copyrighted work upon the parts of instruments serving to reproduce mechanically the musical work, any other person may make similar use of the copyrighted work upon the payment to the copyright proprietor of a royalty of 2 cents on each such part manufactured, to be paid by the manufacturer thereof....

[75] NIMMER, *supra* note 3, at 442.1. Nimmer notes, *id.* at 442:
The motion picture industry has never relied upon the compulsory license provision for the purposes of its sound tracks. Therefore, instead of paying 2 cents for each motion picture film print containing a sound track upon which is recorded a musical composition, motion picture producers obtain a synchronization license, sometimes paying very considerable sums for this right.
The musical compositions referred to here, of course, are those additional to music composed specially for source films.

> ... it relies on a "species of the genus motion picture" analysis in order to assert the non-amenability of soundtracks to the compulsory license. Any theory which erodes the applicability of the compulsory license to soundtracks by employing "species of the genus" notions on an *a priori* basis, is incapable of then positing the inapplicability of section 1(e) as authority for the species of the genus approach.[76]

Clearly, the criticism is well made. Similarly, any theory which seeks to deny the copyrightability of half of a copyrightable motion picture, by directing attention to that half alone without regard to the intellectual legitimacy of the tactic of isolation for analytical purpose, cannot be taken seriously unless and until the conceptual act of isolation can be legally justified. Thus, the path opened by the introduction of *White-Smith* as anti-protectionist support emerges as circular. It leads the concerned analyst back to confrontation with the dominant considerations of copyrightability itself. And what emerges at best from anti-protectionist theory is not yet a formidable theory at all, but rather a valuable indication of a conceptual frame in which theory may be tested once the frame has been corroborated by law.

As we approach that corroboration and test while emerging from this overview of the conflict, both the practical and substantive parameters of our journey rise prominently from the initial analysis undertaken. It is evident that protectionist theory raised solely on *a priori* legal perceptions and extra-judicial opinions will not escape assault so as to regain the mantle of orthodoxy it has lost. It is equally evident that anti-protectionist theory based upon arbitrary aesthetic distinctions and suspect tactical maneuvers will do much to confuse the issue of soundtrack protection, nothing to clarify that issue, and very little toward reducing protectionist theory to a hollow. Moreover, if clarification of the soundtrack copyrightability issue is to come, it would be advantageous, and perhaps even terminally productive, to separate new mythology from old history. Further, if we must seek beyond the proofs of history, it would appear sensible to assume that a legitimate path to legal clarity begins somewhere in the midst of "species of the genus" doctrine. Finally, wherever that path may lead, it is evident that it may not be followed within an analytical vacuum, as attending that doctrine is at least a mandated consideration of the *White-Smith* copyrightability tests, and perhaps a mandated consideration of "reasonableness" as well. As to this conceptual frame, it may be noted that a matrix bounded by "reasonableness" and *White-Smith*

---

[76] Yuzek, *supra* note 2, at 41.

considerations would appear to be an agreeable frame in which to assume that the "species of the genus" doctrine operates. For "reasonableness" analysis and visual appreciability/intelligibility tests, underlaid by notions of legislative intent and aesthetic distinction which remain to be verified, have been the polar tools most frontally waved by antiprotectionist theorists. There can be little objection if these tools are used precisely and are then seen to construct rather than to dismantle.

Be that as it may, the maelstrom of "species of the genus" analysis, bordered potentially by reason and certainly by *White-Smith*, and resting beyond or within the impact of history, may now be entered.

II. *TOWARD AN AFFIRMATION OF SOUNDTRACK COPYRIGHTABILITY*

(A) The Matter of An Original Legislative Intent

If there is one notion which the protectionists and the anti-protectionists accept as axiomatic, it is the supposition that soundtracks as adjuncts to motion picture visual tracks did not exist and were not even in contemplation at the time of the Townsend Amendment, and therefore could not have been comprehended directly by the grant of motion picture copyright. The agreement in the matter of "silent films", "talkies", and the intervening legislative action is quite astonishing. For, etymologically curious though it may be, it is well established in motion picture histories that "silent films" were never silent, and that "talkies" did not remain all-talking for very long.

The motion picture was actually invented by Thomas Edison and his assistant, William Dickson, as a visual-aural mechanism. The following summary of the birth of the new art form denotes what was technologically as well as aesthetically contemplated from the outset:

> In 1888, after more than a decade of experiment, Edison produced the phonograph, an instrument for recording and playing back sound on wax cylinders. He had already seen the motion photographs of [Eadweard] Muybridge, and the idea of combining moving pictures with sound seems to have been in his mind even before the perfected phonograph was offered to the public. In fact, his first efforts in this direction consisted of a strip of small photographs wrapped spirally about just such a cylinder. "Everything should come out of one hole," Edison maintained. When this failed, Edison turned the project over to Dickson—and with it a new film base developed by George Eastman.... It was Dickson who solved the mechanical problem of moving [the film] through the camera, devising the sprocket system that is still stan-

dard on 35mm film today. Indeed, this ingenious man even managed to link up the pictures with the phonograph, demonstrating the Kinetoscope to his employer on October 6, 1889, with a brief film in which Dickson both appeared and spoke. What was in all probability the first actual presentation of a motion-picture film also marked the debut of the talkies![77]

Edison patented the Kinetoscope in 1891. His first commercial efforts were not directed toward film projection, but rather toward popularizing the Kinetoscope as a penny-in-the-slot "peep show" attraction. In 1893, he momentarily put aside the sound aspects of the Kinetoscope and began producing one-minute-long film loops to supply the Kinetoscopes of the "peep show" parlors which became prevalent in the United States by 1894. Other inventors quickly designed projectors to accommodate these film loops. For a few years these film loops, portraying brief incidents like a kiss, an execution, or an on-rushing locomotive, intrigued the public. The novelty wore off rapidly. Before the turn of the century, a bored American public had deserted the "peep show" parlors, and the film loops had been relegated to the oblivion of one-minute vaudeville acts—ones which cleared the vaudeville houses for the next show.[78] Since the vaudeville houses sported pit orchestras, it became general practice for the film loops to be accompanied by orchestral music as they ran.[79]

Meanwhile, the Kinetoscope, unprotected abroad,[80] impressed a number of inventors in England, France, and Germany, who promptly invented equivalent machines of their own. The most important of these was the Cinematograph, a machine which took, printed, and projected pictures. The Cinematograph was perfected in France by Louis and Auguste Lumière.[81] The Lumière Brothers immediately conceived of commercializing the new art form in visual-aural terms. When the Lumière Programme debuted in a Paris basement cafe on December 28, 1895, the program was accompanied by music played on a piano.[82]

In addition to exhibiting their film projections with musical accompaniment, the Lumière Brothers also attempted to add sound effects to their program. In 1896, the Lumière Programme was given its first public performance in Great Britain, accompanied by music played on a harmonium. To imitate engine noises for a scene in the program subtitled

---

[77] A. KNIGHT, THE LIVELIEST ART 16-17 (1957). [hereafter, KNIGHT.]
[78] *Id.* at 17-23.
[79] Limbacher, *How It All Began*, in FILM MUSIC 13, 14 (J. Limbacher ed. 1974).
[80] When Edison patented the Kinetoscope, he neglected to pay the additional $150 fee that would have secured international protection. KNIGHT, *supra* note 77, at 17.
[81] *Id.*

"The Arrival of a Train in a Station", a cylinder of compressed air was used. During the same year, various music halls in England ran film projections, for which the music hall orchestras provided full musical accompaniment.[83]

Back in France, Georges Méliès, "without question the movies' first creative artist,"[84] introduced the narrative, or story-telling, film. All of the films of Méliès were accompanied by musical scores. In fact, the earliest piano scores still extant are those written for the films of Méliès during the last years of the 19th century.[85] Méliès' films were very popular in France—so popular that soon they were being shown in America. Here they were widely seen through the first decade of the 20th century. From the time of their introduction in this country, they ignited public interest in the motion picture art as a narrative medium. They also convinced American producers that sound accompaniment and a running time substantially longer than one minute were indispensable to successful commercialization of the motion picture.

As early as 1900, film makers were experimenting with recording discs to give their films their necessary sound. The first commercialized attempt of this nature apparently took place in England in 1900.[86] Shortly afterward, various phonograph synthesizers were developed in England (in 1904) and in the United States (in 1907) to be used in film exhibition, the films being limited in running time by the playing time of the recording discs.[87] Hundreds of these synchronized films appeared during this period, often produced by music halls or opera companies. However, the quality of their synchronized sound was poor, and the elaboration and advancing popularity of the motion picture soon made it necessary for the productions to incorporate "live" sound provided by piano and/or orchestra.[88]

---

[82] R. MANVELL & J. HUNTLEY, THE TECHNIQUE OF FILM MUSIC 17 (1957). [hereafter, MANVELL & HUNTLEY].
[83] *Id.*
[84] KNIGHT, *supra* note 77, at 24.
[85] Bernstein, *What Ever Happened to Great Movie Music?*, HIGH FIDELITY, July, 1972, at 55. [hereafter, Bernstein.]
[86] The film was entitled "Little Tich and His Big Boots"; a phonograph record was used to give the film its sound. MANVELL & HUNTLEY, *supra* note 82, at 17.
[87] *Id.* at 17 n.1.
[88] *Id.* Professor Knight explains further in KNIGHT, *supra* note 77, at 145:
> Until about 1912 inventors persisted in their efforts to join together sound and visuals, going so far as to run endless belts from the projector motor through the entire length of the theater to a phonograph installed behind the screen. But they soon discovered, as houses continued to grow larger, that the problem was one not merely of synchronization but of amplification as well. The ordinary talking machine simply could not produce the volume of sound required to fill an entire auditorium.

Thus, the piano player and often the orchestra became as uniformly necessary to film exhibition as the projectionist. The first original orchestral score that we have a record of, variously dated at 1907 or 1908, was composed by Camille Saint-Saëns for "L'Assassination du Duc de Guise" in France.[89] In America, the first "suggestions for music" sheets of which we have a record were issued in 1909 with films made by Thomas Edison's company.[90] In 1913, *The Sam Fox Moving Picture Volumes* were published in the United States, offering pieces for film pianists compiled by J. S. Zamecnik.[91]

What was the state of motion picture production, exhibition, and art in 1912 as Congress considered the Townsend Amendment? The following summary is on point:

> The year 1912 was the beginning of the greatest and most prosperous era in the history of the American amusement industry....
>
> Nothing that happened in the rapidly expanding world of musical comedies, operettas, and vaudeville was comparable, however, to the breath-taking development of the silent movies. The men who became the giants of the film industry were beginning to produce films on a large scale in Hollywood. Big movie theaters were erected, not only in New York but in every town and village. This was of tremendous consequence to the music business. The silent film needed music to bring it to life.
>
> "On the silent screen music must take the place of the spoken word" had become one of the credoes of the film industry. Huge theater orchestras were hired to play in the movie palaces of the big cities, and smaller ensembles, trios, or simply an organist or a pianist, were employed in thousands of towns and villages.[92]

Before we consider the specific matter of legislative contemplation, it must be noted that as Congress met to consider the Townsend Amendment, and for many years thereafter, the underlying musical works of this primitive motion picture sound were either incapable of receiving copyright protection or did not need copyright protection independent of that being claimed. Early in 1912, the first of the large "cue sheet" music publishers went into business to meet the huge demand for motion

---

[89] MANVELL & HUNTLEY, *supra* note 82, at 18.
[90] *Id.*
[91] *Id.* at 212.
[92] Winkler, *The Origin of Film Misic*, in FILM MUSIC 15, 15-16 (J. Limbacher ed. 1974).

picture music.[93] These organizations were staffed by hosts of composers specializing in film music. Their "cue sheets" were registered and published like any other musical compositions; the film music publishing houses made their money by supplying enough "cue sheets" to cover every print of every film produced by every film producer for many years following 1911. Moreover, the demand for "cue sheets" soon grew so staggering that many of the publishing houses no longer had to register much of their "cue sheet" music because, as one practitioner of the art of the era put it:

> In desperation we turned to crime. We began to dismember the great masters. We began to murder the works of Beethoven, Mozart, Grieg, J. S. Bach, Verdi, Bizet, Tchaikovsky, and Wagner—everything that wasn't protected by copyright from our pilfering.[94]

This manner of providing sound for motion pictures changed radically toward the end of the 1920s. Experiments in linking film projections with sound on recording discs did not end entirely in 1909, but rather continued on a special attraction basis[95] until, in 1926, the Bell Telephone Laboratories developed a special turntable and 13" to 17" records large enough to produce continuous recorded sound for an entire reel of film. Later that year, Warner Brothers, a major film company facing bankruptcy at the time, invested its remaining assets to aquire the novel sound process, which it named Vitaphone.[96]

Warners first used the Vitaphone process to produce short novelty attractions; a selection of these shorts was premiered with recorded musical scores in August, 1926. Audiences were interested but not excited. In 1927, Fox Films, another major film company, acquired the rights to a German process by which sound could be photographed directly onto

---

[93] *Id.* at 20.
[94] *Id.* at 22.
[95] *E.g.*, "Dream Street" ('15), directed by D. W. Griffith, was presented in New York with a battery of synchronized records of music. MANVELL & HUNTLEY, *supra* note 82, at 212. Ambitious experiments without phonograph records included Griffith's "Birth of a Nation" ('15), which featured a long score performed by live orchestra in major city engagements. KNIGHT, *supra* note 77, at 35. During showings of "Birth of a Nation", paid "noisemakers" were often stationed behind the screens to produce sound effects. Limbacher, *supra* note 79, at 15.
[96] KNIGHT, *supra* note 77, at 146.

film itself.[97] Later that year, Fox released sound-on-film novelty shorts, added music-on-film to its feature film production, and introduced the first sound-on-film newsreels. However, the public did not enthusiastically embrace the new sound film until October 6, 1927, when Warner Brothers released the first feature length "talkie" with a star personality: "The Jazz Singer", starring Al Jolson.[98]

The term "talkie" has been much abused by the courts and commentators in this area. Strictly speaking, "talkies" were "all-talking" movies, so named because "[t]hey just never stopped talking!"[99] In the world of "talkies," the camera was no longer seen to move and the music was no longer heard to sound; the microphone and the sound technician dominated movie making. The popularity of the "talkies" immediately caused the collapse of all the "cue sheet" music publishing houses. Tremendous stocks of film music became worthless overnight.[100]

However, the public enthusiasm for "talkies" lasted little more than a few years. Audiences quickly grew tired of movies which did nothing but talk. By the early 1930s, film producers had realized that the sound-on-film picture was unacceptable commercially and artistically so long as it did nothing but talk. Swiftly, the sound technician was made subservient to the film director, the camera was liberated, and music was reinstated in films.[101] The era of the "talkies" was over, and the era of a mosaic sound-on-film art had begun.

---

[97] The development of the German sound-on-film process actually antedated the development of Vitaphone. Moreover, the German sound-on-film process appears to have antedated another sound-on-film process, called Phonofilm, which was developed by Lee De Forest several years before Vitaphone was developed. Beginning in 1923, De Forest presented his phonofilms as novelty attractions in vaudeville theaters throughout the United States. Inexplicably, these first sound-on-film movies produced little stir in the motion picture industry. *Id.* at 145-46.

[98] *Id.* at 147. For the next three years, the film industry's universal embrace of recorded sound coincided with a struggle for dominance between the proprietor of the sound-on-disc system and the proprietors of various sound-on-film systems. A "patents pool" arrangement ended the competition, and by the end of 1931 sound-on-film was standard. *Id.* at 150.

[99] *Id.* at 143.

[100] Winkler, *supra* note 92, at 24.

[101] This reinstatement bore an important musical shift. At first the film companies turned for the necessary film music to the music publishers they had dealt with beginning in 1912. The catalogs of the "cue sheet" publishers immediately rose in value as tremendously as they had recently dropped in value. Putting music back into films in this manner became so expensive that soon the film companies found it more economical to hire their own composers to write original film scores tailored to the needs of individual films. Thus appeared the film composer and the film score as we know them today. *Id.* at 24-25.

Roughly forty years separate the invention of the motion picture as a visual-aural art and the perfection of the motion picture as a visual-aural art. The action of Congress extending copyright recognition to the motion picture art occured almost exactly halfway through this approximately forty year period of development. Quite clearly, it may not be asserted that the visual-aural character of the art was not contemplated by 1912, for nothing but such a character had been contemplated since the invention of the new art form. It is perhaps true that soundtracks as technological adjuncts to visual tracks could not be specifically foreseen in 1912; yet the technological antecedents of soundtracks—the recording discs employed with phonograph synthesizers and the live musical accompaniment—were not only in contemplation by 1912, they were in proliferate existence for twelve years prior to 1912. More importantly, the aesthetic continuity of a commercialized visual-aural motion picture art remained intact in this country at least from 1900 onward, and was therefore the only aesthetic ambience of that art of which the members of the 62nd Congress could have been substantially aware. Due to the technologically primitive manner in which this aesthetic ambience was produced, via "canned" visual track projection and live or independently recorded musical sound, the visual track was judicially protectible as a photograph and the musical compositions were protectible as physically registered and published music, before and while Congress considered a specific grant of copyright protection to the motion picture. What, then, may be said about Congress' contemplation of the matter?

If we are to be logical, we would have to expect that the 62nd Congress, while not collectively quite sure about how the motion picture would develop technologically, saw itself as protecting something other than, or at least potentially other than, a mere photograph, which was, of course, already recognized by statute.[102] However, perhaps even this rudimentary aesthetic perception is too much to attribute to the 62nd Congress. As one commentator has noted:

> ... Congress in its 1912 enactments to include motion pictures as a copyrightable class failed to even review and change other sections of the copyright law in order to make them compatible with the new class, thereby evidencing little legislative thought about what it was doing. As a result, today we are called upon to fit motion pictures into the language of other sections of the copyright law inapplicable to motion pictures, such as what constitutes the "best

---

[102] This class was first included in 1865 by 13. Stat. 540.

edition" under the deposit requirements of section 12 or what is "twice the amount of the retail price of the best edition" insofar as the failure to deposit under Section 13.[103]

Actually, the bulk of legislative thought relative to the Townsend Amendment was directed to the capacity of motion pictures to infringe. The report of the House Committee on Patents relative to the Townsend Amendment noted that the production of films had grown into a business of vast proportions, necessitating a definite recognition and protection for the films themselves.[104] The dialogue on the floor of Congress was chiefly concerned with protecting the film producers from the hazard of bankruptcy, such a threat being alive so long as an inadvertently infringing film could be exhibited numerous times by numerous exhibitors within a short time period, thereby tolling multiple infringements and auguring unlimited recovery against one film producer.[105]

Thus, in bringing motion pictures into the copyright statute, the Townsend Amendment also embraced additions to the copyright law having a relation to motion pictures only to the extent of the film's capacity to infringe. Just as section 5 was amended to incorporate subsections (1) and (m), section 11 was amended to provide for the deposit of dramatico-musical compositions as well as the deposit of motion picture prints.[106] Section 25 was also amended to limit the recovery available against a motion picture company which inadvertently infringed a copyrighted dramatic or dramatico-musical work.[107] That a motion picture might infringe a dramatico-musical work without actually infringing the musical aspect of the dramatico-musical work is entirely possible: an example would occur where a dramatic film appropriated the storytelling element of an opera without appropriating its musical effects.[108] However, to the extent that the framer of these amendments considered the capacity of the motion picture to infringe a dramatico-musical work, the following exchange on the floor of Congress during the discussion of the amendments provides interest:

---

[103] Brylawski, *supra* note 1, at 360.
[104] H.R. Rep. No. 756, 62d Cong., 2d Sess. 1 (1912); S. Rep. No. 906, 62d Cong., 2d Sess. 1 (1912).
[105] H.R. Rep. No. 756, 62d Cong., 2d Sess. 3-4 (1912); S. Rep. No. 906, 62d Cong., 2d Sess. 3 (1912). *See* 48 CONG. REC. 8288-92 (1912).
[106] Act of Aug. 24, 1912, 37 Stat. 488, *amending* 17 U.S.C. §§5 & 11.
[107] Act of Aug. 24, 1912, 37 Stat. 488, *amending* 17 U.S.C. §25.
[108] An opera is perhaps the most obvious example of a dramatico-musical composition. *See* LATMAN, *supra* note 11, at 26.

TOWARD AN AFFIRMATION 33

> Mr. Mann: There has been at different times considerable controversy with reference to the copyright on musical reproductions. What effect will this change have on that, if any?
>
> Mr. Townsend: It enlarges the scope embraced within that classification. Heretofor, I believe, the classification has been "dramatic or musical productions." There is now recognized, I think, in the theatrical world a third class of performances, commonly known as "dramatico-musical." This amendment makes the manufacturers of motion pictures or other infringers of copyright liable in the case of the infringement of a dramatic or musical or dramatico-musical performance.[109]

Mr. Townsend's statement is perhaps capable of meaning different things to different people. However, when we note that the motion picture of 1912 and even much earlier was entirely capable of infringing the musical as well as the dramatic effects of a dramatico-musical composition, and when we consider that Mr. Townsend was thinking in "performance" terms about the particular infringement issue, the impression emerges distinctly that sound as well as sight was on the mind of the man who brought the motion picture amendments before the 62nd Congress. As to what was on the minds of the other members of that Congress, we know only the historically obvious: if they had seen commercially exhibited motion pictures of the day at all, they had experienced an art form combining sight and sound, irrespective of what transient manner in which the visual was combined with the aural.

If we are to be reasonable, then, we must impute to the 62nd Congress an intention to protect the motion picture art to the extent that the aesthetic distinctions of that art permeated congressional awareness at the time of statutory recognition and mandated continued aesthetic unity after statutory recognition. That would appear to be the heart of any action undertaken as a function of the power "To promote the Progress of Science and useful Arts...."

But *must* we be reasonable, and *is* that the heart of an action extending copyright recognition? Further, if such perceptions are valid, do they operate whether we rest on a protective legislative intent or proceed to "species of the genus" analysis itself? Let us see if our instincts are not only salutory but also mandated by law.

(B) The "Species of the Genus" Doctrine
It is apparent from our earlier discussion that a "species of the genus"

---

[109] 48 CONG. REC. 8289 (1912).

theory of copyrightability has been born of a body of judicial thought meandering enough to lend itself to malleable and therefore divergent treatment in the commentaries. Since application of the doctrine may be crucial to resolution of the soundtrack copyrightability question, a searching examination of the doctrine is demanded if the *Page* court's protective application of the doctrine to motion picture soundtracks is to be identified as valid law rather than as too generous dictum. Such an examination should rightfully proceed on the assumption that the "species of the genus" theory possesses structure in addition to substance, for it is through structure that substance may most readily be identified.

It was suggested earlier that a "reasonableness" maxim might prove as much a wing of such structure as requisite *White-Smith* considerations, and hence, that a conceptual frame established by these two poles might emerge as the legal path by which a "species of the genus" analysis should proceed. The question which initially presents itself here, then, is singular. Is such a conceptual frame the structure in law through which credence may be given to a "species of the genus" copyrightability analysis in a federal statutory sense?

We have noted two cases wherein a "species of the genus" theory was applied in a motion picture context: the decision in *Page*, where copyrightability was not an issue, and the decision in *Edison v. Lubin*, where copyrightability was an issue. Only in *Edison* did the court pay specific deference to an implicit "reasonableness" maxim. In holding a motion picture consisting of one continuous film sequence (*i.e.*, an unedited, one-camera position film loop) copyrightable as a photograph, the court identified the motion picture itself as a photograph since it was "a picture produced by photographic process."[110]

---

[110] *Edison v. Lubin*, 122 Fed. 240, 242 (3d Cir. 1903).
[111] *E.g.*, Meagher, *Copyright Problems Presdented By a New Art*, 30 N.Y.U. L. REV. 1081, 1085 (1955).
[112] The *Edison* court, at 122 Fed. 242, reasoned as follows:
>To say that the continous method by which this negative was secured was unknown when the act was passed, and therefore a photograph of it was not covered by the act, is to beg the question. Such construction is at variance with the object of the act, which was passed to further the constitutional grant of power "to promote the progress of science and useful arts." When Congress, in recognition of the photographic art, saw fit in 1865 to amend the act of 1831 ... and extend copyright protection to a photograph or negative, it is not to be presumed it thought such art could not progress, and that no protection was to be afforded such progress. It must have recognized there would be change and advance in making photographs, just as there has been in making books, printing chromos, and other subjects of copyright.

TOWARD AN AFFIRMATION

However, to note only that the *Edison* court looked at the "sameness" of the process by which a film loop and a photograph are produced[111] is to misconstrue the dominant strain of the *Edison* court's analysis, for the *Edison* court looked to the Constitution to resolve *what to do* about this "sameness" of the new art and the old within a copyrightability setting. And it was through that perception that the *Edison* court decided what to make of the matter of legislative intent—a making seemingly bound to the constitutional charge by reason.[112]

The *Edison* decision was sanctioned two years later in *American Mutoscope & Biograph Co. v. Edison Mfg. Co.*,[113] just as the *Page* dictum was given further credence ten years afterward in *Jerome v. Twentieth Century Fox-Film Corp.*[114] In *American Mutoscope* the issue was whether a motion picture consisting of multiple film sequences (*i.e.*, an edited, multiple-camera position film) was copyrightable as a photograph. The court held that it was, citing *Edison* for support. However, unlike the *Edison* court, which had discussed the "sameness" of the motion picture and the photograph in terms of the physical process by which both had been created, the court in *American Mutoscope* discussed this "sameness" in terms of the "light-written" manner by which the motion picture and the photograph expressed ideas, thoughts, and conceptions so as to come within the constitutional identification of "writings."[115] This aesthetic dimension of the court's constitutional awareness of the manner in which to pose a copyrightability question also appears to have been rooted in the substantive underpinnings of *Edison*. Like the court in *American Mutoscope*, the *Edison* court cited the United States Supreme Court decision in *Burrow-Giles Lithographic Co. v. Sarony*[116] in support of its decision as to what to do within a copyrightability setting with a new art extension of the old. The impact of *Burrow-Giles* in this setting, particularly via the idea-

---

[113] 137 Fed. 262 (C.C.D.N.J. 1905).

[114] 67 F. Supp. 736 (S.D.N.Y. 1946), *aff'd*, 165 F.2d 784 (2d Cir. 1948).

[115] After defining a "writing" in the constitutional sense, the *American Mutoscope* court noted that "if a photograph be not only a light-written picture of some object, but also an expression of an idea, or thought, or conception of the one who takes it, it is a writing within the Constitutional sense, and the proper subject of copyright." 137 Fed. at 265. Continuing, *id.* at 266, the court stated that it was:
> ... unable to see why, if a series of pictures of a moving object taken by a pivoted camera may be copyrighted as a photograph, a series of pictures telling a single story like that of the complainant in this case, even though the camera be placed at different points, may not also be copyrighted as a photograph. Though taken at different points, the pictures express the author's ideas and conceptions embodied in the one story.

[116] 111 U.S. 53 (1884).

tional character it confers upon the "reasonableness" factor of "species of the genus" copyrightability analysis, may be momentarily reserved for subsequent discussion. We now note that to the extent the *Edison* and *American Mutoscope* courts embraced a "reason of the thing" thinking, it was a "reason of the copyright protection" motif of constitutional proportion that underlay their analyses.

The decision in *Jerome v. Twentieth Century Fox-Film Corp.*, sanctioning the *Page* analysis itself, falls outside of motion picture copyrightability analyses in which what might be called "reasonable relations" of an ideational and/or legislative sort have arguably been sought. However, the *Jerome* court, like the *Page* court, was equally determined to be reasonable, if only in dictum. In *Jerome,* the plaintiff argued that the defendant motion picture company had not acquired any right to use the plaintiff's musical composition in defendant's motion picture. The court found that the defendant did acquire such a right from the plaintiff. Though this finding in and of itself disposed of the plaintiff's suit,[117] the court felt compelled to consider certain defenses pleaded by the defendant. One of these was the assertion that the plaintiff's failure to file a notice of use in accord with the compulsory license requisite of section 1(e), after the plaintiff had previously licensed others to use the musical composition in motion pictures, constituted a complete defense to any suit for copyright infringement, in accord with section 1(e).[118]

Though the *Jerome* court considered the point in dictum, the issue was considered by the court to be "so novel and important"[119] that the music publishers and songwriters were permitted to file a brief amicus curiae through counsel for their associations. Agreeing with the claim that the motion picture soundtrack is not the type of mechanical reproduction to which the compulsory license provision of section 1(e) applies,[120] the court stated:

> It was not intended that motion picture films should be in the same class as mechanical reproductions. Since "talkies" have been pro-

---

[117] With one qualification: the plaintiff, in alternative argument, requested and was denied a finding of forfeiture as to rights acquired by the defendant. 67 F. Supp. at 737-38.
[118] 17 U.S.C. §1(e) reads in appropriate part:
It shall be the duty of the copyright owner, if he uses the musical composition himself for the manufacture of parts of instruments serving to reproduce mechanically the musical work, or licenses others to do so, to file notice thereof, accompanied by a recording fee, in the copyright office, and any failure to file such notice shall be a complete defense to any suit, action, or proceeding for any infringement of such copyright.
[119] 67 F. Supp. at 740.

duced commercially, we have had the decision in the *Page* case interpreting the Act as to motion picture rights. There has been no amendment of the Act to deal separately with "talkies," because they are so clearly of the genus "motion pictures."[121]

The willingness of the courts in *Edison* and *American Mutoscope* directly, and in *Page* and *Jerome* in dictum, to look for "reasonable relations" when faced with a motion picture copyrightability question, or to *be* reasonable when considering the issue of motion picture rights, perhaps should not automatically be equated with the necessity of following a "reasonableness" maxim when applying the "species of the genus" theory to the soundtrack copyrightability issue. Yet, as a line of authority implicating such a maxim, these motion picture cases should not be taken lightly. Nonetheless, it has been noted that whatever form of "species of the genus" analysis may be generated by law, the application itself of that analysis may be seen to fall into two distinct categories:

> ... the cases dealing with this general question of reading a copyright statute upon a subsequently developed art fall into two classes: those in which it is sought to hold that activities in the new art may constitute an infringement, under the statute in question, of a copyrighted work of an older art of recognized copyrightability; and those in which it is sought to hold that a work produced by the new art is itself copyrightable under the statute.[122]

Thus, as in the *Page* and *Jerome* cases, the courts have employed the "species of the genus" theory to decide copyright matters which fall outside the narrow realm of copyrightability itself. Moreover, the courts have been so demonstrably reasonable about using "species of the genus" notions in "new art infringement" cases as to invite the suggestion that

---

[120] The *Jerome* court noted that a distinction between mechanical recordings (music rolls, phonograph records, *et al.*) and motion pictures had been drawn in the legislative history attending the Townsend Amendment. *Id* at 742, *citing* H.R. Rep. No. 756, 62d. Cong., 2d Sess (1912). The court did not specify where that distinction appears in the House Report. The court may have been referring to the House Committee's note that the Townsend Amendment would not affect the compulsory license provision of section 1(e). H.R. Rep. No. 756, 62d Cong., 2d Sess. 2 (1912); S. Rep. No. 906, 62d Cong., 2d Sess. 2 (1912). The court may also, or alternatively, have been referring to the House Committee's note that the motion picture amendments would not operate as a compulsory license. *Id.* at 4; S. Rep. No. 906 at 3.

[121] 67 F. Supp. at 742.

[122] Meagher, *supra* note 111, at 1082.

"reasonableness" enters the structure of "species of the genus" doctrine *only* when "new art infringement", and not "new art copyrightability", is in issue.

Thus, in *Rossiter v. Hall*,[123] it was held that the plaintiff's copyrighted engravings had been "copied" when the defendant produced and sold photographs of these engravings, thereby infringing the plaintiff's exclusive rights attending the copyrights owned. The plaintiff's rights were claimed under an Act of 1831. Photographs had recently been extended statutory recognition under an Act of 1865. The defendant argued that his photographs could not "copy" the plaintiff's engravings under the Act of 1831 because the art of photography had not been known when that statute was passed. In denying the defendant's claim, the *Rossiter* court noted that to hold otherwise would work to repeal the protection accorded by copyright law in many cases.[124] The unreasonableness of such a result was further considered when the court noted that since the protection against infringing copying extended to photographs by the Act of 1865 was dependent upon the construction of the language of the Act of 1831, the construction given to the Act of 1831 was necessary to render protective effect to the Act of 1865.[125]

In *Kalem Co. v. Harper Bros.*[126]—relied upon by the *Page* court as authority for its application of "species of the genus" theory to sound-on-film motion pictures—the United States Supreme Court held that the plaintiff's exclusive right to dramatize a novel had been infringed by the defendant's manufacture and sale of a motion picture version of that novel. The plaintiff's rights were claimed under an Act of 1891. Motion pictures were not to receive legislative recognition as copyrightable until a year after *Kalem* was decided, and it is not likely that Congress was aware of the existence and future of Mr. Edison's invention by 1891. The Court, noting the purpose of the statutory clause extending the exclusive right to dramatize,[127] and after discussion of the aesthetic fluidity of a

---

[123] 20 Fed. Cas. 1253, No. 12,082 (C.C.E.D.N.Y. 1866).

[124] The *Rossiter* court noted that books could be reproduced as easily as engravings by a photographer, and that books, therefore, would emerge as unprotectible as engravings if the defendant's argument was accepted. *Id.* at 1254.

[125] The *Rossiter* court noted that the Act of 1865 extended protection to photographs by providing that the provisions of the Act of 1831 be extended to apply to photographs. *Id.*

[126] 22 U.S. 55 (1911).

[127] The Court noted that "[t]he law confines itself to a particular, cognate and well known form of reproduction," *id.* at 63, such that it protects against a reproduction in the form of action.

"dramatization",[128] brought the defendant's activities within the terms of a right defined before motion pictures were known beyond the laboratory.

Language immediately suggestive of a mandated "reasonableness" approach to "new art infringement" cases began to appear with the decision in *Jerome H. Remick & Co. v. American Automobile Accessories Co.*[129] In this case the plaintiff argued that its exclusive right to perform a copyrighted musical composition publicly for profit had been infringed by the defendant's commercial radio broadcast of that musical composition. The plaintiff's rights were claimed under the Act of 1909, enacted before the radio was developed. The court held that the plaintiff's exclusive right had been infringed by the defendant's radio broadcast, reasoning that:

> ... the statute may be applied to new situations not anticipated by Congress, if, fairly construed, such situations come within its intent and meaning. [The court then noted earlier recognitions of this proposition, citing *Rossiter v. Hall.*] While statutes should not be stretched to apply to new situations not fairly within their scope, they should not be so narrowly construed as to permit their evasion because of changing habits due to new inventions and discoveries.[130]

Both the decision and rationale of *Remick* were given specific sanction by the United States Supreme Court in *Buck v. Jewell-LaSalle Realty Co.*[131] In this case the plaintiff's exclusive right to publicly perform a copyrighted musical composition was held to have been infringed by the defendant hotel proprietor's installation and use of a radio receiving set and loudspeakers in his hotel, where the defendant's patrons could be entertained by radio broadcasts of the plaintiff's musical composition. In view of the earlier decisions in *Kalem* and *Remick*, the defendant did not contend that radio broadcasting could not be brought within the scope of the Act of 1909, under which the plaintiff claimed his rights. Rather, the defendant argued that no two or more performances could be perceived within a single rendition of a copyrighted musical composition, since Congress could not have been aware of the possibility of effecting multiple performances from a single rendition when the 1909 statute was passed. Rejecting this argument, Mr. Justice Brandeis noted a judicial

---

[128] The Court confined its analysis to the manners by which "drama may be achieved by action" without speech. *Id* at 61.
[129] 5 F.2d 411 (6th Cir. 1925).
[130] *Id.* at 411.
[131] 283 U.S. 191 (1931).

duty of reasonable construction relative to the statutory construction issue before the Court.[132] Both *Kalem* and *Remick* were cited as authority for the derivation of this duty.

While *Rossiter, Kalem, Remick,* and *Buck v. Jewell,* by virtue of their frontal concern with "fair constructions" and "protective duties", lend considerable weight to the argument that a "reasonableness" maxim inheres in proper "species of the genus" analysis, they perhaps fail as an additional line of authority to lend conclusive weight to that argument, for the "reasonableness" maxim they espouse operates within this line of authority only as to a "new art infringement" issue. Despite the "reasonable relations" of a constitutional dimension frontally identified in *Edison v. Lubin* and *American Mutoscope* within a "new art copyrightability" setting, it has been suggested that the "reasonableness" maxim employed in "species of the genus" analysis by the courts in *Rossiter, Kalem, Remick,* and *Buck v. Jewell,* "while appropriate to prevention of new-art 'evasions' of the rights in recognized copyright subjects, is not particularly applicable to the new-work-copyrightability question"[133] itself.

However, no reason has been offered as to why that approach may be deemed inappropriate in a "new art copyrightability" setting. More importantly, what evidence we have other than that provided by the motion picture cases already noted suggests not only that the "reasonableness" maxim is as appropriate in a "new art copyrightability" setting as in a "new art infringement" setting, but that it is as mandated by law in the copyrightability context as in the infringement context.

Surely there has been no erosion of a "reasonableness" approach when a "species of the genus" analysis has been applied in cases which fall into a third class distinguishable from the two previously noted: those in which it is sought to hold that a newly copyrighted art itself is infringed as to rights claimed to arise under statutory language enacted prior to the development of the new art. Such cases arise when the section 1 general enumeration of rights is not appropriately amended to accommodate a section 5 amendment extending new art copyrightability. Since the legis-

---

[132] Mr. Justice Brandeis stated, *id.* at 198:
> ... nothing in the Act circumscribes the meaning to be attributed to the term "performance," or prevents a single rendition of a copyrighted selection from resulting in more than one public performance for profit. While this may not have been possible before the development of radio broadcasting, the novelty of the means used does not lessen the duty of the courts to give full protection to the monopoly of public performance for profit which Congress has secured to the composer.

[133] Meagher, *supra* note 111, at 1086.

lative treatment accorded motion pictures in 1912 provides a classic instance in which such a lapse led to *sui generis* treatment under the Copyright Act, it is not surprising to find that the better known cases of this class are, in fact, motion picture cases.

Thus, in *Tiffany Productions, Inc. v. Dewing*,[134] *Metro-Goldwyn-Mayer Distributing Corp. v. Bijou Theatre Co.*,[135] and *Universal Pictures Co., Inc. v. Harold Lloyd Corp.*,[136] it was held that a motion picture photoplay was a "dramatic work" as that term is used in section 1(d), and that plaintiff proprietors of various copyrighted motion picture photoplays were entitled to invoke the protection of section 1(d) to prevent unlicensed exhibition, performance, or reproduction. The courts in *Tiffany* and *Metro* rejected the argument that section 1(d) was inapplicable to motion picture photoplays because motion pictures were not commercially known when the Copyright Act was passed in 1909. Both courts cited *Kalem* and Mr. Justice Brandeis' "reasonableness" thesis in *Buck v. Jewell* in support of their holdings. The *Tiffany* decision was expressly approved by the First Circuit in *Metro* and later by the Ninth Circuit in *Universal*.

The *Metro* disposition underwent an evolution worth noting. The case was remanded after decision by the First Circuit,[137] whereupon the defendants' argument was again rejected, again on authority of *Buck v. Jewell* and *Kalem*.[138] However, the district court also found another reason why the defendants' argument was without merit. In one of the few instances where film history was judicially examined to glean legal relevance in a "species of the genus" setting, the district court took judicial notice of the development of the motion picture from 1888 to 1908 and concluded that motion pictures were commercially known prior to 1909.[139] The attention to "reasonableness" in "species of the genus"

---

[134] 50 F.2d 911 (D. Md. 1931).
[135] 59 F.2d 70 (1st Cir. 1932).
[136] 162 F.2d 354 (9th Cir. 1947).
[137] The First Circuit's protective holding applied to motion picture photoplays. The court was not called upon to decide whether the unlicensed exhibition of a motion picture other than a photoplay would infringe any section 1(d) rights. Since the original bill of complaint drawn by the plaintiff motion picture proprietors did not identify the specific type of motion picture as to which infringement was alleged, the First Circuit set aside a district court decree dismissing the plaintiffs' bill of complaint and remanded with direction to allow any desired amendment to the bill. 59 F.2d at 76-77.
[138] Metro-Goldwyn-Mayer Distributing Corp. v. Bijou Theatre Co., 17 U.S.P.Q. 124 (D.C. Mass. 1933).
[139] *Id.* at 130.

statutory construction exhibited by the various courts in these "new art infringed" cases may best be summarized by the First Circuit's statement in *Metro* that:

> The copyright statutes ought to be reasonably construed with a view to effecting the purpose intended by Congress. They ought not to be unduly extended by judicial construction to include privileges not intended to be conferred, nor so narrowly construed as to deprive those entitled to their benefits of the rights Congress intended to grant.[140]

The "new art infringed" cases are clearly more analogous to "new art copyrightability" cases than to "new art infringement" cases. For in "new art infringement" cases, the courts have been concerned with new art evasions of the rights attending other copyright subjects, while in "new art copyrightability" cases and in "new art infringed" cases, the courts have been concerned with protection of the new art itself. Yet, contrary to the assertion of a dichotomous "species of the genus" approach to statutory construction, a "reasonableness" maxim has operated as forcefully in the "new art infringed" cases where the concern was new art protection, as it has operated in the "new art infringement" cases where the concern was new art evasions of the rights in recognized copyright subjects. It would seem, then, that the same maxim should also operate in the field in which *Edison v. Lubin* and *American Mutoscope* indicate that it holds equal sway —in "new art copyrightability" cases, where new art protection is entirely at issue.

Before further exploring the tenability of this position, it may be appropriate to ask: if "reasonableness" may be shorn from "species of the genus" statutory construction in "new art copyrightability" cases, what, then, shall be its analytical replacement? Reference was made earlier to the anti-protectionist suggestion that a purely physical symmetry between genus and species might dispose of whatever reasonable legal construction is called for in application of the "species of the genus" theory within a copyrightability setting. That suggestion was identified as suspect when noted because a physical symmetry analysis cannot alone dispose of whatever constitutional problem inheres in "species of the genus" analysis. As we have seen, the courts in *Edison v. Lubin* and *American Mutoscope* employed physical symmetry to identify an aesthetic symmetry by which the early motion picture, like the photograph, could be considered a light-written "writing". Correspondingly, as to statutory construction of the

---

[140] 59 F.2d at 76.

motion picture amendments, the visual/visual-aural nature of the physical symmetry posited in anti-protectionist theory is historically insupportable, at least aesthetically. It is extremely unlikely that the members of the 62nd Congress ever saw a motion picture without sound accompaniment. Hence, both genus and species of aesthetic concern here are arts enjoyed as sight and sound experiences, the species being distinguished from the genus only by virtue of the technological attachment of sight and sound.

Nevertheless, the physical "sameness" quotient appears to be the agreeable replacement for reason where a dichotomous rule of "species of the genus" statutory construction has been urged. For, independently of but in accord with the physical symmetry position, it has been argued that:

> One might therefore conclude ... that the rule concerning copyrightability of a new work under a pre-existing statute stands as follows: where the new work is the result of an "advance" in an old art, the products of which had had recognized copyrightability under the statute, but is still basically the product of the same "processes" as the recognized class of works, the fact that the statute was enacted prior to knowledge or development of the "advance" will not bar copyrightability of the new work; but, where the new work is not the result of such an "advance" or "new development" in the old art, nor an "extension of the old processes," but rather the product of methods "entirely original and independent" of the recognized arts, the new work cannot be brought under the old-art terms of copyrightable subjects in a statute passed before knowledge and development of the new methods.[141]

The problem with this analysis is that it mistakes the trees of physical process for the forest of copyrightability concerns. Certainly physical symmetry may be identified as *a* concern of "species of the genus" copyrightability analysis. Yet to say that it is the determinative factor of

---

[141] Meagher, *supra* note 111, at 1085. The rule proposed by Meagher is compounded from a reading of Wood v. Abbot, 30 Fed. Cas. 424, No. 17,938. (C.C.S.D.N.Y. 1866), as well as a reading of Edison v. Lubin. In Wood v. Abbott it was held that a photograph was not copyrightable as a print or an engraving under a pre-existing statute; thus, the plaintiff's photographs could not be protected from the defendant's copying as "prints, cuts, or engravings" under the terms of the antecedent statute. There is neither physical symmetry nor aesthetic symmetry between the art of photography and the arts of printing or engraving. The *Wood* court's discussion of the radical differences between these arts began with a denial of physical symmetry and ended with a denial of aesthetic symmetry. *Id.* at 425.

that analysis is to turn a mere utility into an analytical tool of little legal value to the analyst. Physical symmetry, for instance, cannot override the failure to meet *de minimis* requisites of copyrightability, no matter how identical the creative processes involved, no matter how same the "sameness" claimed.[142] Physical symmetry would rather appear to be a valuable consideration in "species of the genus" copyrightability analysis only when used to identify an aesthetic symmetry which springs from the basically similar manners in which old and new art processes are employed to project the "writings" of "authors". That would harmonize the utility of physical symmetry with the core consideration of copyrightability itself. That is also precisely the use made of physical symmetry in *Edison v. Lubin* and *American Mutoscope*.

Such use is special, however, for it mandates the application of reason in a "species of the genus" copyrightability analysis. Indeed, just as there can be no ideational concern in copyright law without an aesthetic concern, there can be neither ideational nor aesthetic concern in a "species of the genus" copyrightability analysis without an application of reason. In this regard, it must not escape notice that all copyrightable subjects are nothing less than "species" of the "genus" identified as "writings" in the Constitution—a statute enacted substantially prior to the technological development of many subjects later deemed copyrightable. When that is remembered, it may be conclusively established that a "reasonableness" maxim has been part and parcel of "species of the genus" copyrightability analysis since the implicit inception of that analysis. No lengthy turning of the judicial pages of copyright history is necessary to prove the point.

The courts in *Edison v. Lubin* and *American Mutoscope* supported their searches for "reasonable relations" of a constitutional dimension with reference to *Burrow-Giles Lithographic Co. v. Sarony*, where the congressional grant of copyright protection to photographs in 1865 was upheld as constitutional. In *Burrow-Giles*, a unanimous United States Supreme Court identified photographs as one of the classes of literary productions embraced by the term "writings", as that term is used in the Copyright Clause of the Constitution, and as that term was construed by Congress in 1790 and later in 1802. The constitutional identification operated at least in so far as photographs represented "original intellectual conceptions",[143] and despite the fact that the art of photography was entirely unknown as late as 1802. It is well known that the boundary between the new art and "writings" was measured in *Burrow-Giles* by the

---

[142] The *de minimis* rule pervades all classes of copyrightable subject matter. LATMAN, *supra* note 11, at 19.
[143] Burrow-Giles Lithographic Co. v. Sarony, 111 U.S. 53, 58 (1884).
[144] *Id.*

TOWARD AN AFFIRMATION

application of reason to statutory construction, and that this boundary was closed by positing an embryonic aesthetic symmetry among the various manners "by which the ideas in the mind of the author are given visible expression."[144]

That this "reasonableness" motif has assumed the force of an analytical maxim in the practice of copyrightability analysis is quite demonstrable. Judicial condonation has consistently been accorded to the congressional expansion of copyright to embrace new art expressions of the ideas of "authors".[145] Moreover, that this "reasonableness" maxim most appropriately takes the form of a "reasonable relation" search of aesthetic character in "species of the genus" copyrightability analysis was the apparent thesis of Judge Learned Hand. In *Reiss v. National Quotation Bureau, Inc.*[146] it was held that a code book containing a large number of coined words having no known meaning, but aesthetically and practically useful once adapted to convey an agreed meaning via cable correspondence of ideas, was a "writing" under the Constitution. Rejecting the defendant infringers' argument that certain English cases favorable to the plaintiff's cause were distinguishable because they arose under an act of Parliament which was not limited by any Constitution, Judge Hand stated:

> So, indeed, they were, and if our Constitution embalms inflexibly the habits of 1789 there may be something in the point. But it does not; its grants of power to Congress comprise, not only what was then known, but what the ingenuity of men should devise thereafter. Of course, the new subject-matter must have some relation to the grant; but we interpret it by the general practices of civilized peoples in similar fields, for it is not a strait-jacket, but a charter for a living people.[147]

If, on authority of *Burrow-Giles, Reiss, Edison v. Lubin,* and *American Mutoscope*, we must accept the "reasonableness" maxim as a structural wing of the "species of the genus" analysis applied in a "new art copyright-

---

[145] *E.g.,* note the continuum of judicial sanction in the field of photography following the *Burrow-Giles* decision: American Mutoscope & Biograph Co. v. Edison Mfg. Co., 137 Fed. 262 (C.C.D.N.J. 1905) (*see* note 115 *supra*); Pagano v. Chas. Beseler Co., 234 Fed. 963 (S.D.N.Y. 1916) (photograph of street scene and public building, taken after creative decision making, is a "writing"); Jewelers' Circular Pub. Co. v. Keystone Pub. Co., 274 Fed. 932 (S.D.N.Y. 1921) (every photograph must be a "writing" because no photograph, however simple, can be unaffected by personal influence of photographer).
[146] 276 Fed. 717 (S.D.N.Y. 1921).
[147] *Id.* at 719.

ability" context, we may properly inquire as to the direction by which a responsible "reasonable relation" inquiry should proceed. Since there are two genus/species patterns which have emerged from copyrightability analyses of the past, it would appear that two relationships are of independent or correlative importance in seeking to fashion rules of copyrightability analysis.

When the statutory "genus" is contained within the Constitution ("writings"), and a newly developed "species" is claimed to rest constitutionally within a protection announced by Congress, then a simple rule of reason operates. In this case, the newly developed "species" may be identified with the statutory "genus", to the extent the aesthetic distinctions of the newly developed "species" render it reasonably compatible with both the traditional judicial construction of "writings", and the constitutional mandate "To promote the Progress of Science and useful Arts...." Such was the relation of the idea-expressing photograph in *Burrow-Giles,* and of the aesthetically or practically useful code book in *Reiss,* to "writings" and to the promotive/protective constitutional charge.

When, however, the statutory "genus" has already been identified as a "species" itself, of the constitutional "genus" called "writings", and as a legitimate effectuation of the promotive/protective constitutional charge, and a newly developed "species" is claimed to assume the protection legislatively accorded the antecedent "genus", then a somewhat different rule of reason operates. In this case, the newly developed "species" may be identified with the antecedent "genus", not only to the extent its aesthetic distinctions render it reasonably compatible with the antecedent "genus", but also to the extent the "reason of the copyright protection" accorded the antecedent "genus" would be undercut or nullified unless the newly developed "species" is embraced within the copyright protection accorded by statute to the antecedent "genus". Such was the relation of idea-expressing, light-written motion picture to idea-expressing, light-written photograph in *Edison v. Lubin* and *American Mutoscope.*

Clearly, application of the second rule guards fully against mitigation of any protective effect established by application of the first rule. The point may be illustrated in motion picture terms when we consider that in denying protection to the dialog tracks and/or the music tracks of a motion picture, we may also eliminate the protection covering much of the idea-expression of the motion picture work, and thereby remove that work from the category of "writings" as it was presented by its "author" to lie therein. If the aesthetic distinctions of a motion picture, when its soundtrack or solely its music tracks are deemed unprotectible, render the motion picture no longer as fully compatible with a "writing" as it was when intact, or no longer fully compatible with the constitutionally charted protection extended by Congress to motion pictures, then the newly developed "species" (motion pictures with soundtracks) must be identified with and embraced within the statutory protection accorded the antecedent "genus" (motion pictures without soundtracks). Given the stated condition, that result must follow, unless we are to nullify the congressional grant and render meaningless the promotive/protective constitutional charge vis-à-vis motion pictures. The alternative does not in any way commend itself to reason. Since it is "reasonableness" that we have seen to form one wing of the framing structure of "species of the genus" copyrightability analysis, the alternative would not be available, at least in the context of a *legal* "species of the genus" copyrightability analysis.

As was noted earlier, that "reasonableness" is by logic a requisite of "species of the genus" copyrightability analysis has been at least sensed in anti-protectionist circles. As is now evident, there is by law very little "perhaps", no mere "falling back", and much more than "fairness" to the casual copyrightability suggestion: "Perhaps it is fair . . . to fall back upon the reason of the thing."[148]

However, we have not yet examined the extent to which the motion picture may be disemboweled as to its ideational distinctions by severing its sound from its visuals. It was suggested elsewhere, remember, that one could look responsibly at "the reason of the thing" and *at least* deem the motion picture music tracks unprotectible. That is an aesthetic concern. That concern has not been transposed to any aesthetic analysis supportive of the anti-protectionist claim. It has not previously lent itself to appropriate aesthetic analysis here. Yet that analysis may lie at the heart of a constitutionally proper soundtrack copyrightability inquiry. As to its legal implications, it may be our largest responsibility to undertake that analysis.

As we pass into such a confrontation, several salient implications arise from the preceding analysis which can bear conceptual fruit only after our aesthetic examination has been made. We have seen that a "reasonableness" maxim is as mandated a legal consideration in "species of the genus" copyrightability analysis as are the copyrightability tests of *White-Smith*. Our question as to this framing structure of "species of the genus" copyrightability analysis was initially posed as singular. With our answer in tow, another question emerges now and will be considered shortly.

We may ask: what relationship, if any, exists between the "reasonableness" maxim and the *White-Smith* tests when the "species of the genus"

---

[148] *See* text accompanying note 61 *supra*.

theory is applied to a copyrightability issue? As to the motion picture soundtrack copyrightability issue, we have already had more than a hint of a relationship of compatibility between these two poles, for both "reasonableness" and "intelligibility" notions derive most understandably from aesthetic perceptions, be they the courts' or Congress', and as they were derived in *Burrow-Giles* and *Reiss*.

But if there is indeed a relationship between the two poles when the "species of the genus" theory is applied within a copyrightability setting, may it be one of interaction as well as of compatibility? Of this we have had a strong indication also. The denial of motion picture copyrightability to an isolated motion picture visual track, as a potential function of the denial of motion picture copyrightability to an isolated motion picture soundtrack, would not be a result commending itself to reason, though the twin denials be based on *White-Smith* analyses which might appear to be proper in themselves.

However, whatever the dimensions of the anticipated relationship, it is through aesthetic analysis that we may come to appreciate any identified bridge, and it is to motion picture aesthetics that we now turn.

(C) *The Aesthetic Identity of the Motion Picture Soundtrack*[149]

"Music," as Judge Hand noted in *Reiss*, "is not normally a representative art."[150] A distinguishing characteristic of film music, however, is that it is always a representative art—and one which operates visually as well as aurally. For that reason, film music has often been identified as the only new form of music to have been developed in the 20th century. Since their evolution from "peep show" curios to narrative art during the final years of the 19th century, movies have simply never been without music. Can it be, as anti-protectionist theory at its bottom line would have us believe, that such a new form of music, entirely bequeathed by the motion picture art, has made no material contribution to the integrated motion

---

[149] Since the importance of the dialog tracks incorporated in the film soundtrack has been conceded in anti-protectionist theory when a look at the "reason of the thing" is deemed fair, it is unnecessary to explore that importance when "reasonableness" is seen to be mandated. We deal here, then, only with the importance of the music tracks incorporated in the film soundtrack. Moreover, even within the context of a music track analysis it appears unnecessary to explore the aesthetic identity of on-screen vocal numbers or off-screen songs, since the relationship of lyricised music to dialog or narration is obvious. Thus, the aesthetic identity of the dramatic orchestral music incorporated in the film music tracks emerges as our only necessary concern with the aesthetic identity of the motion picture soundtrack.

[150] Reiss v. National Quotation Bureau, Inc., 276 Fed. 717, 718 (S.D.N.Y. 1921).

picture art, but rather has served extraneously to merely enhance the enjoyment of that art? If aesthetics must be considered frontally—and indeed they must when aesthetic distinctions are claimed, without benefit of aesthetic analysis, to deny copyrightability to part of an artistic unity—then here we shall delve into aesthetics to attain that most subjective of copyright identifications: the aesthetic explanation.

For the legal analyst, however, it is hardly the most familiar of intellectual sojourns. As one writer in the area has noted,[151] describing the values and functions of the mysterious art of combining moving pictures with music is rather like describing a beautiful woman—if it must be done fully, it cannot be done adequately. If, then, the aesthetic analysis is to be achieved in reasonably precise fashion, it is perhaps best to allow those who understand that mysterious art most fully—and who share with their employers the most to lose should the aesthetic claims of anti-protectionist theory be adopted judicially—speak for both their musical art and their role in a motion picture art. That shall be the format employed here.

A recognition of the indispensability of music to film—not as to all films, but rather as to the aesthetic arsenal of film making techniques from which all films are selectively constructed so as to present "ideas" in cinematic fashion—can arise only as a function of the basic recognition of the film art as a mosaic art. As to the creative distinctions of the motion picture, that was the concept urged by George Méliès in France before the turn of the century and refined by D. W. Griffith in America after the turn of the century.[152] For three quarters of a century that concept has not been questioned in film theory; yet now we find it denied in legal theory. As to the role of music within that art, we shall let a film historian introduce our analysis, lest the explanations of film composers which follow appear self-serving to the uninitiated.

> At its most general level, film music serves as a kind of cohesive, filling in empty spaces in the action or dialogue—this is neutral,

---

[151] T. THOMAS, MUSIC FOR THE MOVIES 17 (1973). [hereafter, THOMAS.]

[152] *See* KNIGHT, *supra* note 77, at 23-37. Note that expressions of this mosaic concept evidence the degree to which the mosaic nature of the film art is cherished by film artisans. *E.g.*, director King Vidor speaks of "an indelible oneness about music and film," K. VIDOR, KING VIDOR ON FILM MAKING 145 (1972), and notes: "...I do know that cinema embraces all the arts and brings them all to her ample bosom." *Id.* at 142. Composer Ralph Vaughan-Williams identified the disposition of the film composers when he averred that "the film contains potentialities for the combination of all the arts such as Wagner never dreamt of." Johnson, *Face the Music*, FILM QUARTERLY, Summer, 1969, at 3, *quoting* R. Vaughan-Williams.

background music and the composer's most ungrateful job since it must enliven and colour scenes without drawing attention to itself.

Film music must also build a sense of continuity, uniting the visual parts—this is most important because a theatrical film is like a jig-saw puzzle. The most obvious example of this is the cinematic montage—a cascade of varying shots that would be chaotic without some unifying musical thought.

Something else that skilful scoring can accomplish is underlining the theatrical build-up of scenes, pinpointing various emotions and actions, and then rounding it off with a sense of finality. In this sense, music is a definite story-telling device. Another aspect of this device is that of utilizing "source music," that is, music that can be seen on the screen—coming from a radio, or a record player or from a dance band, a circus, a cafe or an actor playing an instrument.

On a higher level of accomplishment, film music can do two greatly important things (how well depends on the composer). One: create an atmosphere. Two: colour the tone of the picture. Atmosphere music can be quite obviously geographical or historical, placing the story in a certain locale at a certain time with certain kinds of people in certain kinds of situations, but it's a test of the composer's knowledge and imagination how well he does this.

.... This is the psychology of scoring, being able to shade emotions, to lighten or darken moods, to heighten sensitivities, to imply, to suggest, to define character and refine personality, to help generate momentum or create tension, to warm the picture or cool it, and—most subtle of all—to allude to thoughts that are unspoken and situations that remain unseen. Such music plays upon the minds of the audience.[153]

The most familiar musical device through which this psychology of scoring is achieved is the leitmotif—"a specific theme continually used to identify a specific character, situation, or emotion."[154] Through use of this device, the film makers can project what the visual alone may not project: a specific thought process of a character.[155]

Thus, in Max Steiner's score for "The Informer" ('35), the motivations which drive Gypo Nolan to an act of betrayal (the desire to obtain money to provide passage from war-torn Ireland to America) are repeatedly identified musically. Whenever Gypo stares at a reward poster picturing his friend's face, recognizably American tunes are interjected within an otherwise murking musical atmosphere of Irish character. In "Laura" ('44), the process by which the detective falls in love with a woman he believes to be dead is demonstrated musically. Throughout the first

---

[153] THOMAS, *supra* note 151, at 17.
[154] Bernstein, *supra* note 85, at 56.

half of the film, Laura exists in the present only by virtue of her portrait and her representation in David Raksin's music. In "A Place In the Sun" ('51), the murderous impulses which stir within George Eastman are not described by dialog prior to the climactic "murder". Rather, composer Franz Waxman represents these impulses with "low-pitched, regularly accented eighth notes that [are] readily recognizable whenever they occur...."[156] The terrors and guilts imbedded within Blanche DuBois' tragic past are central to an understanding of her disintegration in the final scenes of "A Streetcar Named Desire" ('51). Until that disintegration occurs, its dramatic justification enters the structure of the film musically, through Alex North's fracturing interjection of the "Varsouviana" (capped by an echoing gunshot) within an otherwise piercingly delicate musical fabric.

Most films depend upon the use of the leitmotif to some extent to present ideas which cannot be—or which have not been elected to be—otherwise expressed. It is not surprising, then, to find the leitmotif employed as a central element in the structure of the film often described as the greatest film ever made.

"Citizen Kane" ('41) operates on many intellectual levels, and not the least of its successes is this film's achievement as mystery. Indeed, every dramatic element of *Kane* springs from the cinematic use of artifice—the search for the meaning of "Rosebud". This meaning is made obviously evident at the very end of the film as the camera approaches the furnace at Xanadu to discover that little sled before it is consumed by fire. However, no mystery succeeds as mystery unless the solution has been made elliptically evident long before it is made obviously evident. It was director

---

[155] There is also an accepted language by which the motion picture camera may identify some specific thought processes of a character, but that language is much more limited in this respect than is the language of film music, which, *with* the visual, can explore a wide range of character thoughts. *E.g.,* Professor Sarris notes, in A. SARRIS, THE AMERICAN CINEMA 55 (1968):
> The opening, wordless sequences in *Rio Bravo* ['59] present all the moral issues of the film. The low-angle shot of [John] Wayne looking down at [Dean] Martin with sorrowful disdain tells the audience all it has to know about the two men, and [director Howard]Hawks even tilts his camera to isolate the relationship from its background and to intensify the reciprocal feelings of shame and disappointment.

It is important to note that there is only so much that one can do with camera positioning vis-à-vis the thoughts of characters, and that even then music is often employed with the camera to identify the thoughts. In "Rio Bravo", for instance, the opening camera shots described above are accompanied by suspended, dissonant musical chords.

[156] Hendricks, *Film Music Comes of Age,* in FILM MUSIC 45 (J. Limbacher ed. 1974).

Orson Welles' intention to identify "Rosebud" at the very beginning of the film—but subtly. Thus, as the film begins, with the camera passing above a "No Trespassing" sign to descend upon the voluminous contents of Xanadu, composer Bernard Herrmann deploys twin leitmotifs to identify, through the scoring, the two central ideas of the film: the unspoiled innocence of Kane's childhood ("Rosebud"), and its antithesis, Kane's consumptive lust for power throughout his maturation ("Kane's Ambition"). The "Ambition" motif is played against the "Rosebud" motif, the latter entering the structure of the film at this point to indicate that "Rosebud" itself is buried within the debris seen on-screen, the former entering in counterpoint to note that Kane's whole adult life has been lived in contradiction of the ideal represented by "Rosebud". Then, as Kane dies on-screen and the audience is given to wonder what a fading collossus thinks of as he expires, all of the musical motifs and atmospheres of Kane's childhood are presented on the soundtrack. Minutes later, in the first of many flashbacks through which Kane's life story is told, Kane is shown as a child playing with his sled in the snow, while the "Rosebud" motif is boldly and lyrically developed in the scoring. And so, in one of many similarly constructed scenes of this film, the music of "Citizen Kane" assumes its position as a major part of the ideational structure of the movie.[157] Without its music, *Kane* is virtually a digest version of the artistic whole.

It is unnecessary to examine every foot of "Citizen Kane", or of any other film, to determine just how much a part of a film's ideational content music can be and often is. The initial point, it is assumed, has been made by reference to one enduringly famous example. Leitmotifs are not always necessary to the structural fabric of a film, but music itself almost always is. The composer of "Citizen Kane" explains why:

> The real reason for music is that a piece of film, by its nature, lacks a certain ability to convey emotional overtones. Many times in many films, dialogue may not give a clue to the feelings of a character. It's the music or the lighting or the camera movement. When a film is well made, the music's function is to fuse a piece of film so that it has an inevitable beginning and end. When you cut a piece of film you can do it perhaps a dozen ways, but once you put

---

[157] The limited "Citizen Kane" analysis offered here has been drawn from, and explanations of other scenes in "Citizen Kane" may be found within, the following: Palmer, *The Classic Film Scores of Bernard Herrmann* (RCA brochure published with RCA LP ARL 1-0704, 1974); Cook, *Bernard Herrmann*, 18 FILMS IN REVIEW 398 (1967); Gilling, *The Colour of the Music*, SIGHT AND SOUND, Winter, 1971-72, at 35 [hereafter, Gilling].

music to it, that becomes the absolutely final way. . . . .

Music essentially provides an unconscious series of anchors for the viewer. It isn't always apparent and you don't have to know, but it serves its function. I think Cocteau said that a good film score should create the feeling that one is not aware whether the music is making the film go forward or whether the film is pushing the music forward.[158]

Bernard Herrmann's reference to the manner in which the viewer perceives the phenomena of movement and emotionality in film lends itself to exposition by examples. As to the cinematic phenomenon of movement, the following summary is indicative of the aesthetic rationale of this point:

Why does film need background music? As Ernest Lindgren points out in *The Art of Film*, music and film each depend upon the phenomenon of movement, and are thereby allied aesthetically. Second, sound movement reinforces visual movement. Third, and most important, music balances the sensual experience of sight with that of sound, and we are more relaxed when we are not straining to comprehend through one sense alone.[159]

Thus, composer Elmer Bernstein has noted that his initial scoring of the long exodus scene in "The Ten Commandments" ('56), where Moses leads the Hebrews out of Egyptian bondage, was emphatically rejected by director Cecil B. DeMille precisely because the music accurately reflected the pace of the scene, as it had been filmed and edited, with some 8000 extras marching in passive and lumbering fashion. DeMille insisted that the young composer write music for the scene having a much faster pace than that possessed by the isolated visual. The director explained that the visual would then assume the hurried pace and jubilant message of the music. Bernstein rescored the scene as directed, and thereby learned early in his career, and from an experienced teacher, exactly how cinematic energy is achieved. Later Bernstein wrote the music for the slowly paced "The Magnificent Seven" ('60) in tempos always faster than those of the isolated visual. The film thus became one of the most rhythmically vigorous of westerns.[160]

As Composer Leonard Rosenman notes:

You're dealing with two arts that are very similar—sight and sound—both move in time and both require memory for the per-

---

[158] Gilling, *supra* note 157, at 37, *quoting* B. Herrmann.
[159] Embler, *The Structure of Film Music*, in FILM MUSIC 61 (J. Limbacher ed. 1974). [hereafter, Embler.]
[160] Bernstein, *supra* note 85, at 57-58.

ception of organization..... The film composer has to bear in mind that we are a visually oriented society. In fact, it's biological; more of our brain is given to vision than to hearing. Film music should be an analogue to the action of the film, and likewise, the film should become an analogue of the dramatic action of the music. This is the value of a director and composer working together in the construction of the film.[161]

Music has been regarded as especially valuable in achieving a cinematic sense of movement where movement itself is most difficult to achieve in films—in battle scenes, particularly massive ones. Music is almost always used to lend structure, progression, and often meaning to battle footage which, without music, would generally be chaotic and incomprehensible beyond the accepted muscularity of the images themselves. For the visually cumbersome "Battle On the Ice" fought between the Russians and the German invaders in "Alexander Nevsky" ('38), Sergei Prokoviev's music adds terror to the otherwise static approach of the Teutonic knights through the mist, creates an overpowering combative energy as the ancient military forces meet on the ice, and continues almost as the propelling force of the battle itself, until finally it explodes in hymnal thanksgiving to announce that the Grand Duke Alexander has carried the day. Director Laurence Olivier was so intent that the structure, tension, and meaning of the Battle of Agincourt be fully perceived in "Henry V" ('46), that William Walton's music for the scene was given full prominence therein; even sound effects were omitted from the soundtrack during the battle scene. For the longest sustained, most intricately edited scenes of mass warfare yet produced, Dimitri Tiomkin's battle scoring in "The Alamo" ('60) reads like an audio-visual symphony, its successive movements devoted to plunging the audience into various patterns of warfare until the large orchestra, announcing "No Quarter", joins the camera to hurl on-screen enemy army and off-screen audience against and into the famed chapel where the last stand of the wounded is made, where the camera freezes, and where the music ends. So successful is the marriage of sight and sound in this last example, that not only is a cinematic sense of propulsion created, but the creation apparently causes all sense of time to be lost. Though the sequence consumes about twelve minutes of screen time, reviewer after reviewer reported it as encompassing a full hour.

---

[161] THOMAS, *supra* note 151, at 207, *quoting* L. Rosenman. For information about the impact of film music on the human body, in the physiological sense, *see:* Johnson, *Face the Music.* FILM QUARTERLY, Summer, 1969, at 3, 3-5.

This losing of time sense often operates concurrently with the manipulated perception of movement in the motion picture art. It is particularly endemic to films which seek to frighten an audience as well as to create movement within an audience perception. Moreover, the lost sense may take cinematic form as a time contraction as well as a time extension. Bernard Herrmann explains the attention paid this phenomenon in the creation of "Psycho" ('60):

> A scene without dialogue may seen endlessly long by itself, but appears to shorten with the music. *Psycho* has many scenes like this which seemed to take place in a few seconds, but the sequences are quite long. The opposite happens with the shower murder, which only lasts about ten seconds. People will tell you that it goes on for ever, but it's the intensity of the music which makes it seem so.[162]

Movement and timing are so essential to most films, and music is so essential to the manner in which most films achieve movement and timing, that the marriage of sight and sound in this respect is often thought of by film makers to be an extension of the art of ballet.[163] Yet as important as these achievements are to the film art, they are basically sought as means by which an ideational end of emotional dimension may be created. Though not all films are successful in generating an emotional reaction in viewers, one would be hard pressed to cite a film which does not aim at generating a certain emotional impact. For that is the goal most generally identified with art and entertainment, and it is often the manner in which the expression of "ideas" is made manifest and affective. It is as to this emotional dimension of the film art that music again assumes a paramount importance. For instance, it has been noted that:

> Film can show fear or loneliness, but because these are feelings and not acts, the shots depicting them are static. Quite often they cannot be sustained long enough to tell the story. But, by the addition of music, moods can be strengthened and protracted. Thus, music can bring movement when film cannot.[164]

---

[162] Gilling, *supra* note 157, at 38, *quoting* B. Herrmann.
[163] Composer Dimitri Tiomkin explains, in Tiomkin, *Composing For Films,* in FILM MUSIC 55, 58 (J. Limbacher ed. 1974) [hereafter, Tiomkin]:
 There is a much closer affinity between ballet and movies than casual thought suggests. The story is more involved in ballet, for the screen is a more plastic medium, and its story-telling is therefore simpler. Nevertheless, the eloquence of music is as indispensable to film as to ballet. Sometimes I think a good picture is really just ballet with dialogue.
[164] Embler, *supra* note 159, at 62.

So, we find that the grandly romantic spiritual passion which torments Heathcliff, and from which Cathy cannot escape, is continuously evoked throughout "Wuthering Heights" ('39) by Alfred Newman's music. In "The Best Years of Our Lives" ('46), it is through the frightening implications in Hugo Friedhofer's music that the audience immediately recognizes and understands the emotional terrors sparked in the mind of a former World War II bombardier pilot as he sits in the cockpit of a wrecked B-36 after the war has ended. That Emma Bovary's fascination with the aristocratic Rudolph is decidedly sexual is made first elegantly and then fiercely evident during the ball sequence of "Madame Bovary" ('49) by the celebrated waltz which highlights Miklos Rozsa's score, and which undergoes changes in momentum, melodic contour, and orchestral support until the music, like the on-screen dancers, collapses in near frenzied exhaustion. That audiences are able to sympathize with the speechless Kong of "King Kong" ('33) and Frankenstein of "The Bride of Frankenstein" ('35) is due to the music of Max Steiner and Franz Waxman, respectively, which gives voice to the feelings of these inhuman but so humanized beings. Entry into the delicate and mystical world of children's perceptions, rationalizations, fears, and loves, so central to a comprehension of "To Kill a Mockingbird" ('62), is achieved through the guide provided by Elmer Bernstein's exquisitely fragile scoring.

As composer Elmer Bernstein explains on the subject of cinematic emotionality and the role of music in establishing that emotionality:

> The job of the composer is really very varied. You must use your art to heighten the emotional aspects of the film—music can tell the story in purely emotional terms and the film by itself cannot. The reason it can't is that it's a visual language and basically intellectual. You look at an image and then you have to interpret what it means, whereas if you listen to something or someone and you understand what you hear—that's an emotional process. Music is particularly emotional—if you are affected by it, you don't have to ask what it means. [At this point, Mr. Bernstein is asked: Film music is almost an idealization of the visual image?] Yes, even with a subject as kinetic as *The Magnificent Seven*, the moment you translate into music the scene of horsemen riding over the plains it becomes an emotional accompaniment to the action. That's part of the fun of being a film composer, that you are reaching people at a subliminal level, where they are relatively defenseless. That's an exciting thing because you can make people feel a certain way, even though they may not understand why they feel that way.[165]

---

[165] THOMAS, *supra* note 151, at 193, *quoting* E. Bernstein.

This is not to say that music in films does not become an intellectual force in association with the visual, once the rudimentary intellectual visual has been given an emotional character by the attachment of musical sound to light-written sight. As the author of "The Structure of Film Music" explains:

> There is practically no film without music, but the music is *consciously* heard by very few. However, *everybody* hears it unconsciously, and it is undeniable that music helps to shape the concepts and emotions which a film creates in our minds. This is so importantly true that parts of Alex North's music for *A Streetcar Named Desire* were attacked by the Legion of Decency as "too suggestive."[166]

That the emotional impact provided by music in films becomes perceptible in intellectual fashion once music and films are joined, so as to offer an intended ideational content, is so important a fact of film making life that the absence of music, or silence, has long been considered a musical concern of film making itself. The power of film music to project intended ideas also embraces the power to project unintended ideas. Moreover, the projection of what are perceived in some quarters to be dangerous or offensive ideas can arise in either manner. The attempted (and partially successful) censorship of some of the *Streetcar* music is a famous case in point.[167] Other examples are more illustrative of the potential of film to be misinterpreted as to its ideational content by virtue of the use of music.

Thus, the final scene of "The Nun's Story" ('59), in which Sister Luke leaves her religious order, contains no music other than the tolling of a convent bell. The scene had originally been scored by Franz Waxman, the composer on the film, but director Fred Zinnemann removed the finale music from the film soundtrack prior to the film's release. That action was taken because the finale of "The Nun's Story" was considered to be too potentially controversial to be given anything but an ambiguous ideational character. As director Zinnemann later explained, if the music for this scene expressed gloom, the film would imply that it was unfortunate that Sister Luke left the convent. Yet if the music expressed exultation, even an exultation relative merely to Sister Luke's courage, that could be perceived as a corporate act of encouraging nuns to leave the convent.[168]

---

[166] Embler, *supra* note 159, at 61 (emphasis in original).
[167] *See* M. SCHUMACH, THE FACE ON THE CUTTING ROOM FLOOR 71-78 (1964).
[168] *An Interview With Fred Zinnemann*, FOCUS ON FILM, Spring, 1973, at 26.

More recently, composer and UCLA/USC Professor David Raksin was asked why, in view of the obvious musical care he had devoted to the occasionally gruesome "What's the Matter With Helen? ('71), he had allowed the roll-up of cast credits which ends the film to proceed in disquieting silence, when that seemingly would have been the perfect place to voice a postlude of empathy for the slain heroine of the film.[169] Professor Raksin explained:

> Just as it is pointless to extend sympathy to deaf ears (such as those of the dead), it is pointless to try to evoke sympathy unless that is *the purpose of the picture*. . . . [T]here was no question in our minds about that being the way to end the picture, abrupt cut-off and all, and no music for the end cast-titles. As I said, sympathy in such a situation is not only superfluous, it is impossible. To have mourned the dead, or even the bereaved, at that point, would have been to swallow the delusion that sympathy could have made any difference at all. It is, in my mind, questionable enough to "legitimately" manipulate the multiple arts which comprise the film medium without having the gall to butt in when it is better to leave things unsaid.[170]

The use of silence, then, may be seen to be as essential to the structuring of the ideational content of film as the use of music. It should not be surprising, therefore, to note that the decision as to where *not* to employ music in a film is most often left to the composer.[171] It is in this sense that "silence itself becomes a kind of music, and the impact when music stops is as great as when it begins."[172] This is especially true when the relationship of the music on the film's music tracks to the dialog on the film's dialog tracks is considered. For, as composer Bronislau Kaper notes:

> With dialog, the most effective technique is the use of silence, to lull the audience with neutral music into a sense of half security and then to stop when something really important is said—nothing is as loud in films as silence.[173]

The cinematic relationship of music, including the use of silence, to

---

[169] Cook, *What's the Matter With Helen?*, in FILM MUSIC 114, 118 (J. Limbacher ed. 1974).
[170] *Id., quoting* D. Raksin (emphasis in original).
[171] Bernstein, *supra* note 85, at 58.
[172] Rosenthal, *Laurence Rosenthal on the Aesthetics of Scoring Films*, in T. THOMAS, MUSIC FOR THE MOVIES 33 (1973). [hereafter, Rosenthal.]
[173] THOMAS, *supra* note 151, at 90, *quoting* B. Kaper.

dialog, may be seen to have multiple dimensions beyond that noted above. First, music is often employed to make the sound of spoken dialog variant and/or emotionally affective. Second, music is often used in place of dialog. Third, music is sometimes used to deliberately obscure dialog. Fourth, music is sometimes used to contradict what is being said in the dialog. Fifth, music is often used to introduce the movement of an otherwise unseen force while dialog is being spoken.

Just as the interrelationship of sight and sound confers movement, timing, and emotional/intellectual overtones to a motion picture in the manner of ballet, the interrelationship of music-sound and dialog-sound, operating on one side of the sight and sound equation, is often conceived in film theory to derive aesthetically from the art of opera. This may seem curious initially, for dialog is at least more obviously important to the comprehensibility of most films than is music, and thus the film art is sometimes mistaken by non-film makers to be an extension of the art of theater. However, as composer Laurence Rosenthal explains:

> Film, unlike the theater, is essentially a visual-aural rather than a verbal-intellectual medium. Even though the two obviously share certain properties, such as dramatic action, dialogue, and character, the basic nature of the film is quite different.
>
> One of the differences is that, in a film, sound becomes a highly sensory element, whether it be music, sound effect, or speech. Total silence is an unnatural vacuum in a film. The ear seems to insist on filling it—whether with a few harp notes, the rustle of clothing, or a human voice. Of course, a great express train could race by on the screen, accompanied by perfect silence or with its natural sound replaced by that of a plaintive woodwind, and that might be enormously effective, but the point is that some sound —or silence—in relation to preceding and subsequent sounds, seems essential. In principle, dialogue plays a lesser role in the aural complex of a film than it does on the stage, where, of course, it enjoys complete supremacy. Hence the correspondingly greater importance of music and sound in motion pictures.[174]

The first to postulate an operatic equation between film music and film dialog was Erich Wolfgang Korngold, himself a composer of operas and one of the few musical "wunderkinds" of the 20th century.

---

[174] Rosenthal, *supra* note 172, at 34. Rosenthal adds, *id.*:
> I would wish, however, to avoid giving the impression that music is an absolute essential in any film. It is quite possible, for example, to make a dry, hard, factual, journalistic picture which music would completely destroy by softening or theatricalising.

Korngold's experimentation with respect to the operatic equation lay in composing film music just below the pitch of actors' voices. In this manner the composer introduced subtle support to spoken words and infused many a love scene with the emotional impact of an operatic love duet.[175]

Now, it is not generally realized that all human voices have octaves and that these octaves exhibit wide variations in pitch and timbre. Just as music can "soften" or "harden" the faces of actors perceived visually, music can complement the speaking voice perceived aurally so as to give it qualities it does not possess inherently. Dimitri Tiomkin, another film artisan who favors the operatic equation, identifies actors like John Wayne, James Stewart, and Jean Arthur as a film composer's delights, because the voices of these actors have so little color in themselves that their pitch and timbre can be complemented with almost any pattern of instrumentation, thereby lending such voices, when perceived cinematically, a flexibility which surpasses that available in a naturally flexible voice.[176] Composer Leonard Rosenman notes that music deployed with dialog in films "should generate that dramatic excitement which the marriage of the arts . . . should bring about, almost in an operatic sense —except that the 'arias' are spoken rather than sung."[177] These precepts were demonstrated by Rosenman in his music for "East of Eden" ('55), of which the composer notes:

> . . . when scoring under dialogue I took into account that Julie Harris is a high soprano, James Dean is a tenor, and Raymond Massey a bass-baritone. The design of the instrumentation and of the thematic material itself was influenced by consideration of these voice ranges and qualities. Often "holes" were left in the scoring for the voice to be utilized as a sort of speaking instrument.[178]

As important as the complementary function of music vis-à-vis dialog is music's substitutional function vis-à-vis dialog. The decision to eliminate dialog and to let music speak for the actors is made by the film director. Sometimes there is no choice in this respect, as where the central "speaking" character is a Kong, a Frankenstein, or a mute such as the protagonist of "Johnny Belinda" ('48). Where there is a choice, many of the most famous film directors—John Ford and Alfred Hitchcock are

---

[175] G. Korngold, *The Classic Film Scores of Erich Wolfgang Korngold*, (RCA brochure published with RCA LP LSC-3330, 1972).
[176] Tiomkin, *supra* note 163, at 58-59.
[177] Rosenman, *East of Eden*, in FILM MUSIC 86, 87 (J. Limbacher ed. 1974).
[178] *Id.*

exalted examples—have consistently elected to eliminate dialog in favor of exposition by music. As to the manner in which this decision manifests itself artistically, composer Bernard Herrmann explains his association with Alfred Hitchcock:

> You always work with Hitchcock from the beginning, from the time of the script. He depends on music and often photographs a scene knowing that music will complete it. If that is the case, he may eliminate dialogue completely. When we worked on *Vertigo*, he said when we came to the famous recognition scene, 'If we're going to have music, we won't have one word of dialogue; we'll just have the camera and you.[179]

Often the script itself omits dialog at certain points, so as to implicitly demand the use of music to give "speech" to a character in a particular situation to be filmed. Joseph Mankiewicz, the director-writer of "Cleopatra" ('63), noted of Alex North's music for the sequence in that film in which a lone Mark Antony, deserted by his army in payment for his abdication at Actium, silently charges Octavian's army to force an engagement: "As the muted trumpets scream, in Antony's name, for honourable death, they scream an anguish which cannot be written, in a voice no actor can project."[180] In "Ben-Hur" ('59), the script specified that at no time was Christ's voice to be heard in the film. Yet it also called for the sequence in which Christ appears before thousands of listeners to deliver the Sermon on the Mount. What might seem an incongruity to the layman was an effective projection on the part of the film maker. For it be the function of Miklos Rozsa's music during this scene to intimate the words of the sermon. That is precisely what the composer did in this sequence, by ingeniously molding the notes of the Christ motif of the score to the unheard but well-known words of the sermon.

A more rarely deployed but equally powerful use of music in association with dialog is the functional obliteration of spoken words by music. This technique lends itself to a number of sophisticated uses:

> ... such as the devise in *On the Waterfront* of obscuring with Leonard Bernstein's music certain lines of dialogue, emphasizing

---

[179] Gilling, *supra* note 157, at 38, *quoting* B. Herrmann. For further insights into the director/composer working relationship, *see:* Bernstein, *The Annotated Friedkin,* FILMMUSIC NOTEBOOK, Winter, 1974-75, at 10; Goldsmith, *Vital Dialog in Film Making Between Director and Composer,* Variety, May 15, 1974, at 61, col. 4.

[180] Mankiewicz, *Cleopatra* (notes published with 20th Century-Fox LP SXG/5008, 1963).

their intended banality. Here the emotional line of music tells much more than would the obliterated words. In another scene in the same film, sound and music violently drown out the actors to produce an extraordinary feeling of frenzied impotence. The spectator may not be aware of how this is achieved, but he is nevertheless affected by it.[181]

The most daring use of music in films occurs when it becomes the function of the music to either balance or contradict that which the dialog appears to be saying in terms of dramatic thesis. Great artistic risks are involved in using music for these ends; if the composer fails, then the film fails at its most crucial artistic level. For example, it was the thesis of the makers of "Who's Afraid of Virginia Woolf?" ('66) that George and Martha, despite the unrelievedly excoriating words they hurl at each other, actually share a compatible relationship of love underlying the relationship of mutual hatred which operates prominently in the dialog. Thus, it was left to composer Alex North to create a musical ambience for *Virginia Woolf* specifically designed to carry the underlying thesis of the film. North discarded one musical approach after another before he settled upon the quasi-baroque, exquisitely tender music by which this film subtly delivers its most important message. Somewhat similar is the use of music throughout "Farenheit 451" ('66). Here, the characters of a futuristic society are politically repressed from uttering anything but banalities about happiness. What emotions and torments still grace their feelings and thoughts are identified through Bernard Herrmann's omnipresent musical translation.

The use of music to interject movement of an unseen force while dialog is being spoken is so familiar a cinematic device that the more famous examples of this technique have become cues to which audiences respond immediately: the thumping musical effects which grow in thunder to announce the approach of the monster ("King Kong"); the bugles which rise above the visual fracas and the musical fray to signal rescue by the cavalry ("Stagecoach", '39); the chilling mixture of woodwinds and searing strings (Max Steiner) or simply the softly beating drums (Dimitri Tiomkin) which mirrors the pioneers' realization that the Indians are about to attack ("They Died With Their Boots On", '42, and "Red River", '48). A richer use of music for such purpose is offered by the availability of stereophonic recording techniques. Thus, for the sequence in which Brutus commits suicide in the film version of William Shakespeare's

---

[181] Rosenthal, *supra* note 172, at 35.

"Julius Caesar" ('53), the film makers were able to achieve that which Shakespeare might have given his eye teeth to accomplish. Composer Miklos Rozsa explains what, why, and how:

> Throughout these scenes I wanted to give the impression that the victorious armies of Antony and Octavian are continuously advancing and coming nearer and nearer. This scene, however, is the culmination of the tragedy, when its noblest character, Brutus, like a Greek hero in a Greek drama, faces his inescapable fate. I wrote, therefore, two entirely different scores, contrapuntally worked out, but in content completely independent. The one, which represents Antony's nearing army, is a march based on Caesar's theme and is scored for brass, woodwind, and percussion instruments. The other, which plays the scene in the foreground and underlines the tragedy of Brutus, is scored for strings only. Thus there is a complete contrast of color between the two, apart from their emotional, rhythmic and thematic differences. The stereophonic technique, with three loud speakers behind the screen, came to my help. As the direction of the approaching army is from the right corner of the screen, we put the march track on this loud speaker and the string track on the two others, screen center and left corner. Thus there is a complete separation of the two scores, which were recorded separately, and geographically the listener immediately feels that the army is marching from the right corner of the screen. As Brutus dies the march becomes louder and louder and as the servant runs out from the scene it completely overpowers Brutus' string music and dominates the whole screen.[182]

The ideational importance of music in films has thus far been discussed by isolating a number of aesthetic dimensions by which the art of combining moving pictures and music may be understood. When we consider that all of these individual dimensions are interrelated, we reach that level at which film music may be consummately distinguished from all other forms of music. The motion picture art is a narrative art, and film music is one of the linguistic means by which the visual-aural nature of motion picture narration is identified and achieved. The impact of this equation upon so special a form as film music is to aesthetically divorce this particular form of music from that which has generally been considered music throughout centuries previous to the 20th.

As composer Leonard Rosenman explains:

---

[182] Rozsa, *Julius Caesar,* in FILM MUSIC 132, 135 (J. Limbacher ed. 1974).

> [Film music] has all the attributes of music—melody, harmony, counterpoint—but it is something less than music because its motivating pulsation is literary and not musical. Unlike other mixed media forms, such as opera, the composer has no control over the text, over the *mise-en-scène*; he is writing to a circumscribed form.[183]

Whether it be called "something less" or "something more" than "music", there is little doubt that film music is a literary form of music, that it is the representative art which Judge Learned Hand correctly identified "music" itself as normally not being. Composer Jerry Goldsmith probably speaks for most serious composers who have been attracted to the communicative potential of the motion picture art when he says:

> The function of a score is to enlarge the scope of a film. I try for emotional penetration—not for complementing the action. To me, the important thing about music is *statement*.[184]

A recent example of such statement making is provided by "Papillon" ('73), which was scored by Goldsmith. The expository portion of this film ends with the title character surviving a live-or-die escape attempt from a French penal colony. The audience is then informed of the success of the escape attempt, and of the later dissolution of the French penal colony system, the brutalities of this system having been well explored earlier. As the production credits are mounted on-screen, the camera returns to the penal colony and records its decay through the following years as jungle growths swallow it up. Goldsmith's music, so devoted to emotional penetration of human relationships throughout the expository drama, turns extremely harsh for this finale. Unrelated to the preceding scoring except for its summational objective, this finale music simply and totally damns a penal system too inhumane for a civilized nation to tolerate.

That motion pictures make statements, and that music when employed in motion pictures is one of the means by which such statements are made, becomes emphatically clear when it is noted that the films which have made the most classically important statements in the weightiest of fashions have, without exception, employed music as a vital element in the structuring as well as the making of those statements. The great literary themes of what might be called ideological cinema generally fall into two

---

[183] THOMAS, *supra* note 151, at 207, *quoting* L. Rosenman.
[184] THOMAS, *supra* note 151, at 210, *quoting* J. Goldsmith (emphasis in original).

generic categories: the spiritual and the political, both of which operate in humanistic terms.

Such films, being cinematic essays in essence, lend themselves to certain pretensions, but they always adhere to the requisite structure of essay: they make a statement of purpose or theme at the outset, they delve into a long exposition of purpose or theme thereafter, and they conclude with a restatement of purpose or theme. As we have seen, there are any number of ways in which the exposition may be made, and all of the film arts are employed to varying degrees at various moments to achieve this exposition. As to the introductory statement and the concluding restatement, however, only two cinematic devices are available. One is to simply announce, by means of an off-screen voice or an on-screen title card, exactly "what this film is about" and, later, "what this film has been about." The other is to allow the introductory statement and the concluding restatement to be made by musical composition associated with a well planned visual. Since the former technique bears all the earmarks of an inartistic hammering of the head, while the latter can be achieved subtly and emotionally as well, it is the musical narrative which is usually elected. Of course, once this technique is employed, it is then indispensable to the structural integrity of the motion picture.

Thus, in "Quo Vadis" ('51), the opposing ideological forces of the expository drama are forcefully set forth in the prelude by Miklos Rozsa's juxtaposition of antithetical musical forces. Against a visual portrayal of a Roman stone relief identifying the historical stage, a chorus of one hundred—the "Voices of Humanity"—offers a bold musical setting of the words, "Quo Vadis Domine?", and their English translation, "Lord, Wither Goest Thou?". The chorus represents the urging question of Christianity. An orchestra of seventy-five, representative of the raw power of an Imperial Rome under Nero, repeatedly lashes at the chorus with fanfare interruptions. These eventually lock with the chorus in a sustained musical cataclysm. As the prelude rushes to its conclusion, the chorus is heard saliently to overlay the orchestra. Much later, as the film ends, the "Voices of Humanity" return; after reprising the "Quo Vadis Domine?" question, they conclusively answer that question by speaking as the voice of Christ. The words introduce a hymn, and the powerful announcement of spiritual conquest rises jubilantly above the dying fanfares which signify the end of Nero's Rome.

Such musical developments as these represent a highly sophisticated approach toward positing literary statement in films, and many of the recognized masterpieces among film scores themselves derive from this kind of musical confrontation with great spiritual and political events. Ideological cinema itself reached a zenith in the United States in 1960 with the release of a triumvirate of "Armageddon epics": "Spartacus",

"The Alamo", and "Exodus". The ideological aspirations of these three films are political in nature, and the characters of their political statements are virtually identical. All three films deal centrally with the struggle for human freedom and dignity, and all three films basically assert that "the eternal choice of all men— to endure oppression or resist"[185]—must manifest itself as an affirmative act of resistance when the alternative is totalitarian subjugation. Films can hardly make statements more vital to twentieth century experience, and once again such statement is structured and introduced musically.

Thus, in "Spartacus", Alex North's prelude music surges with modern dissonance and brooding harmony, these to announce immediately that although the seventy thousand slaves so brutally crushed in their rebellion against Imperial Rome were ancient slaves, their experience is directly relevant to 20th century experience. As the camera traces the contours of elegantly formed Roman statuary and reliefs, North's martial rhythms are suddenly deployed to posit a liberation theme of heroic stature. The theme representing the pursuit of freedom swells as new orchestral forces are progressively introduced to expand the literary thesis. Finally, the camera lights upon a solitary Roman bust and remains stationary as the music becomes a political force itself. Strident sound patterns flay at the symbolic bust until the head, unable to withstand assault by the massive force of the musical statement, cracks, shatters, and then disintegrates.

In the prelude of "The Alamo", the camera serves up a series of portraits of the famous mission chapel as it looked in 1836. Dimitri Tiomkin's music, meanwhile, subtly and hauntingly posits the meaning of the event associated with this American shrine. The composer first offers an eerie restructuring of the *deguello,* an historically infamous trumpet call descended from the Moors and carried from Mexico to Texas by the dictator Santa Anna, who employed it to signal that no quarter would be given the less than two hundred American men and women who held back an army of many thousands for thirteen days, thus providing the rest of Texas time to organize an army to repel the invasion. In Tiomkin's vision, the *deguello* represents the totalitarian alternative, and thus it becomes the leitmotif by which "the eternal choice of all men" is identified in the prelude and throughout the film. Structurally, its use in the prelude demands an answer in the prelude. Tiomkin's interjection of the nostalgic and deeply moving theme known as "The Green Leaves of Summer" identifies that answer as bearing a character conceived not in terms of a raw and antithetical force, but rather in terms of the love of men for the

---

[185] J. E. GRANT, THE ALAMO (narrative titles 2 of screenplay embodied in Batjac motion picture, 1960).

simple beauties of life—a love directed so centrally to those beauties that it predicates the willingness of men to give their lives so that their families, friends, and neighbors might enjoy that which is personally expendable in the extreme sacrifice. The visuals and music of this prelude consume little more than two minutes of screen time, yet they structure the power to move audiences to tears through one of the quietest but most powerful utilizations of the representative screen arts yet achieved.

The structural prelude of "Exodus" is similar in its emotional impact but entirely singular in its ideological statement. As an empty blue screen suddenly sparkles with the low flicker of the Eternal Light, a towering horn figure announces the theme composed by Ernest Gold to represent the emerging state of Israel. As a large orchestra takes up this theme, the flame, a visual representation of the survival of the Jewish people, begins to grow. As the flame expands and approaches the upper level of the screen, the orchestral forces expand to give the fire a consummate emotional and intellectual import. Finally, the fire entirely consumes the visual. As the screen turns to its brightest hues, a massive orchestra carries the "Exodus" theme toward a crescendo which floods the theater, leaving the audience in no doubt as to the sympathies of the film makers.

There is, of course, an artistic thought process by which composers assume a creative literary posture when they structure all of the statements and posit some of the statements in a motion picture which has something vital to say. The following explanation by the doyen of American film composers, concerning one of the recognized masterworks among film scores, is illustrative. For the scoring of George Stevens' film "The Diary of Anne Frank" ('59), Alfred Newman visited the house in Amsterdam where the Frank family had lain in hiding for so long. Later he reported:

> It was a strange experience—standing in that room where Anne had lived and from where she was eventually led away to die, I had a feeling mixed of exaltation and repugnance. George Stevens had decided that the film shouldn't be one of gloom, but that we should concentrate on the love and humour of these people. During my visit, I had lunch with Anne Frank's father, a charming man, and he wanted to know what my music would be like. I could only tell him in the abstract that what touched me most about the book was its spirituality, and that was what I wanted to say in the music. This seemed to please him. When it came to the actual scoring—I didn't try to illustrate, except in a few places, what was happening on the screen, so much as to invoke in the music the remembrance of happier times, the longings for the future—the longings of an oppressed people.[186]

---

[186] THOMAS, *supra* note 151, at 60, *quoting* A. Newman.

And thus we may ground our perception of what is meant when motion picture analysts assert: "Writing film music is unique in one respect—it is needed, and this is a situation found nowhere else in contemporary musical life."[187]

It has been deemed necessary to offer only an overview of the aesthetic principles of the visual-aural motion picture art, as these principles have been worked out in the practice of that art, and as they have been identified in the literature which seeks to explain that art. In a sense, even this overview constitutes a regrettable trespass. For the achieved motion picture art arises from the interaction of various arts which operate to produce "a wonderful piece of tailoring "[188] in which the stitches are intended to remain unseen and untampered with. As to the contribution of music to that tailoring, it is clear that film music is no less than "the communicating link between the screen and the audience, reaching out and enveloping all in one single experience."[189]

It is of no legal concern, of course, that film music often fails to meet the aesthetic potential of its artistic goals; that is the concern of the film critic and the film music critic, not of the legal analyst weighing copyrightability.[190] Nor does it matter that film music communication may be often perceived unconsciously or sometimes ignored; for "[w]hat a composer does may not be obvious to everyone but that's part of art, that's part and parcel of creativity. . . ."[191]

What are we to make, then, of a legal theory, predicated upon aesthetic distinctions, the distinctions themselves offered without even the remotest recourse to aesthetic analysis, which insists at the least, that the music tracks of a motion picture are immaterial to the artistic integrity or "beneficial use" of the motion picture, and may therefore be severed from the constitutionally charted copyright protection extended to the motion picture and, inclusive of underlying works, fed by the tens of thousands into the public domain?

Apart from the conclusions forced by aesthetic analysis itself, the intellectual arrogance which inheres in an anti-protectionist position so urged would alone appear to mandate dismissal of this odd legal theory. For it is patently absurd to urge the denial of copyrightability to certain stitches necessary to the construction of an artistic tailoring, merely by virtue of the assumption that if these stitches remain substantially unseen,

---

[187] THOMAS, *supra* note 151, at 19.
[188] Gilling, *supra* note 157, at 37, *quoting* B. Herrmann.
[189] Palmer, *Music in the Hollywood Biblical Spectacular*, CHURCH MUSIC, Dec., 1972, at 5, 9, *quoting* B. Herrmann.
[190] *See* LATMAN, *supra* note 11, at 15.
[191] THOMAS, *supra* note 151, at 185, *quoting* A. North.

then they must, in fact, be immaterial to the tailoring itself, and thereby may be uprooted and dispensed with.

It is true that the motion picture art is a subtle and mysterious art. And it is axiomatic that the motion picture art is an art which, to a substantial degree, no longer works its phenomena so consummately if and when it seeks to make the integral elements of its communicative structure self-evident.

Responsibilities, however, do arise, and they are, in this area, not light. As the preceding commentary discloses, the aesthetic distinctions which characterize the motion picture art are not inscrutable. In certain quarters they are well known, and to all quarters their identification is easily available. That which operates at the bottom line of anti-protectionist theory and which is claimed to be reasonable should properly be acknowledged not as a legal theory at all, but rather as a cultural ignorance masquerading as legal theory. As such it may be identified as bearing no intellectual validity and no legal import, for a cultural ignorance posing as legal theory is neither legitimate as aesthetic distinction nor acceptable as a basis for sound copyright law.

The question remains as to the protective features conferred upon the motion picture soundtrack itself, within a "species of the genus" copyrightability analysis, by the legitimate aesthetic distinctions of the visual-aural motion picture art. The appointed consideration rests with the impact and interrelationship of the "reasonableness" and *White-Smith* maxims within a "species of the genus" copyrightability setting, wherein aesthetic analysis has not remained unattended. That appointment may now be kept.

(D) The Impact of White-Smith on "Species of the Genus" Analysis

It was contended earlier that if we are to be reasonable in weighing the issue of soundtrack copyrightability, we must impute to the 62nd Congress an intention to protect the motion picture to an extent which would allow us to deem such copyright protection inclusive of the later developed motion picture soundtrack. That particular use of reason was claimed to flow as a logical imperative sprung from historically identifiable aesthetic perceptions and technological parallels.

The call to reason was next demonstrated to be a legal maxim as well as a logical imperative of "species of the genus" analysis when that analysis is applied to a copyrightability question. However, the application of a "reasonableness" maxim in such a context was not claimed to be limited in direction to the symmetry of aesthetic perceptions or technological parallels which may attend, in historically chartable fashion, the protection of a "species" through legal construction of the legislative intent underlying the copyright protection extended to a "genus". While it has been suggested here that a reasonable construction of the legislative intent underlying the motion picture amendments should alone be dispositive of the soundtrack copyrightability question—whether we proceed to "species of the genus" analysis or not—the luxury of such a dispositive use of reason is not always available in or apart from "species of the genus" analysis itself.

Further, it is arguable, as to the particular copyrightability question presented, that a symmetry founded upon aesthetic perceptions and technological parallels, however historically documented, is yet too slight a hanger upon which to hinge an imputation of protective legislative intent. The full weight of the "reasonableness" maxim thus drew our concern, both to carry our analysis of the "species of the genus" doctrine to its logical end within a copyrightability context, and to identify the parameters of that end should our use of reason in a legislative context be deemed fallible as to soundtrack copyrightability itself.

In this respect, it has been urged here that when the "species of the genus" doctrine is employed to determine the copyrightability of a later developed "species" of an antecedent "genus", application of the "reasonableness" maxim mandates attention to the constitutional fabric which underlies copyright recognition of the antecedent "genus". Such attention was claimed to be required for two reasons.

The antecedent "genus", if legitimately protected by copyright itself, must bear a "reasonable relation" to the constitutional definition of "writings," and to the constitutional mandate "To promote the Progress of Science and useful Arts. . . ." If the "species" may be contained within the protection accorded to the antecedent "genus", then that protection must operate as fully in the case of the "species" as in the case of the "genus"—i.e., the extent to which the classified "writing" is protected must not shift.

Further, when the "species" has sprung from the "genus" in aesthetically symmetrical fashion, attention must then be paid to the consequences of denying to the "species" a containment within the protection accorded to the antecedent "genus". If the "genus" has come to be represented only by production of its aesthetically symmetrical "species", then the denial of functional protection to the "species" undercuts the "reason of the copyright protection" accorded the antecedent "genus". That result effectively nullifies the congressional grant and vitiates the meaning of the promotive/protective constitutional charge.

With these considerations in mind, the aesthetic distinctions of the visual-aural motion picture art were then investigated, not only to test a curious anti-protectionist theory claimed to be reasonable and now identified as irredeemably specious, but also to lay the aesthetic foundation necessary to confront the constitutional dimensions of "species of the genus" copyrightability analysis in the present context.

These constitutional dimensions cannot be deemed slight. If, as the Court in *Burrow-Giles* said, "writings" in the Copyright Clause embraces the various forms of creativity "by which the ideas in the mind of the author are given visible expression,"[192] then the motion picture is constitutionally protectible as a "writing" only if (1) it bears "ideas" of its "author", and (2) these "ideas" are given visible expression. It is the concurrent teaching of *White-Smith* that copyright protection is dependent upon the ability to produce the creative work in the form of "copies"—"copy" being defined in joint terms of visual appreciability and intelligibility.[193] But can *Burrow-Giles* be taken to mean that the sound-on-film motion picture is no longer protectible as a "writing" because the "ideas" of its "author" are given visible expression only when ideational expression is achieved through use of visual and aural coordinates? Can *White-Smith* be taken to mean that the sound-on-film motion picture is uncopyrightable because its isolated soundtrack is not visually appreciable and its isolated visual track is not intelligible? Yes: if we divorce all semblance of sanity from the propulsion of abstract logic forced by analytical maneuvers adopted *a priori*. No: if we decline to violate either the constitutional charge or the congressional will, and instead apply the "reasonableness" maxim of "species of the genus" copyrightability analysis which has been identified as the mandate of law.

It may be noted that *Burrow-Giles* and *White-Smith* do not appear to contradict each other as to their identification of copyrightability concerns. The idea expression of *Burrow-Giles* would seem to relate to the intelligibility motif of *White-Smith* just as the visible expression of *Burrow-Giles* would seem to relate to the visual appreciability notion of *White-Smith*—as equivalent substantive poles of copyrightability analysis. Neither case presents a problem in motion picture copyrightability investigations, so long as it is actually the motion picture that is tested for copyrightability. The aesthetic distinctions of the sound-on-film motion picture are such that the idea expression of a motion picture "author" is imbedded within a mosaic technology which both subsumes the visual and springs its interior interrelationships from the visual.

Thus, the intelligibility of this idea expression presents itself as functionally related not just to the isolated visual track of the motion picture, but to the visually appreciable mosaic integration of motion picture visual

---

[192] Burrow-Giles Lithographic Co. v.Sarony, 111 U.S. 53, 58 (1884).
[193] *See* text accompanying notes 63-65 *supra*.

track and motion picture soundtrack. Conversely, the visual appreciability of this idea expression presents itself as functionally related not to just the isolated soundtrack of the motion picture, but to the intelligible mosaic integration of motion picture soundtrack and motion picture visual track. That, at least, is the aesthetic case. More importantly, that is the legal case if by idea expression and intelligibility, and by visible expression and visual appreciability, *Burrow-Giles* and *White-Smith* refer to the *aggregation* of "ideas" which marks the authorship of a single "writing".

It is apparent that *Burrow-Giles* and *White-Smith* implicitly sanction a concept of full ideational impact in authored expression when it comes to applying copyrightability tests; there would be little deference to the promotive/protective constitutional charge if they did not. At the least these cases are compatible with the concept. A photograph presents the *full* ideational expression of its photographer. A musical composition presents the *full* ideational expression of its composer, at least if the composition is of the non-representative musical character which Judge Learned Hand would call general.

Yet that a full ideational expression of one "author" can be carried in singular technological fashion does not mean that another full ideational expression of a different "author" cannot be carried otherwise. Nor must the latter be denied full protection when it is carried by means of a "species", of mosaic technology, which has sprung in aesthetically symmetrical fashion from a "genus", of singular technology, or even of separate technologies. For the base, against which copyrightability tests are to be applied, logically presents itself as a function of the technology which carries the full ideational expression of an "author".

If, for instance, intelligibility via *White-Smith* and idea expression via *Burrow-Giles* are equivalent substantive poles of copyrightability analysis provided by law, then their applied relationship tête-à-tête would appear to be the mandate of law. Their use in law would be chaotic, however, if that which an "author" expresses as a "writing" is not to be considered the object of a reading for intelligibility.

That it is the full ideational impact in authored expression which is of concern in copyrightability analysis is not only the implication of *Burrow-Giles* and *White-Smith*, it was the stated thesis of Mr. Justice Holmes. Concurring specially in *White-Smith*, Holmes noted that the ground of the constitutionally charted grant of copyright itself is:

> ... that the person to whom it is given has invented some new collocation of visible or audible points,—of lines, colors, sounds, or words. The restraint is directed against reproducing this collocation, although but for the invention and the statute any one would

be free to combine the contents of the dictionary, the elements of the spectrum, or the notes of the gamut in any way that he had the wit to devise. The restriction is confined to the specific form, to the collocation devised, of course, but one would expect that, if it was to be protected at all, that collocation would be protected according to what was its essence.[194]

In *White-Smith,* Holmes drew upon the cruxal definition of a subject of copyright so as to further argue that protection should be coextensive with the invention and its social and commercial value. It was his position that a mechanical reproduction of a collocation of sounds, since it gave meaning and worth to the collocation of written notes invented, should be considered a "copy".[195] The Court's decision rejected Holmes' argument as to the extension of "copy" urged on principle. However, that rejection in no way undercut the definition of a copyrightable subject of expression as "the collocation devised". While Holmes argued for protection of a collocation devised of audible points (sounded notes), the Court limited protection to a collocation devised of visible points (written notes). The latter emerged as protectible because it was intelligible and visually appreciable; the former emerged as unprotectible because it was visually unappreciable, though (presumably) intelligible.[196]

As to our own question, however, we have seen that the idea expression of the sound-on-film motion picture is such that the collocation of concern is composed of visible *and* audible points. The argument therefore arises that if the idea expression of motion pictures means anything in a constitutional sense, it means that intelligibility and visual appreciability tests must be applied to "the collocation devised" by the motion picture "author"—and not to visible or audible points of that collocation held in isolation under an analytical maneuver which, at any given instant, leaves some ideas and half-ideas floating in limbo while other ideas and half-ideas are brought under the double-edged ax of *White-Smith.*

Thus, we find that the authority for applying the *White-Smith* copyrightability tests to "the collocation devised" arises not merely as the dictate of a logic which seeks harmony among different copyrightability considerations, but also as the mandate of a "reasonableness' maxim which is not without constitutional support when operating in a "species of the genus" copyrightability setting. For if "the collocation devised" by the "author" is a "writing" in the sense of that which is copyrightable, then—logically, reasonably, constitutionally—the purported "writing"

---

[194] White-Smith Music Publishing Co. v. Apollo Co., 209 U.S. 1, 19 (1908).
[195] *Id.* at 20.
[196] *Id.* at 17.

must be treated as "the collocation devised" when tested as to its copyrightability.

It is possible, of course, for "the collocation devised" by the motion picture "author" to inhere predominantly in the motion picture visual track. Pre-sound-on-film motion pictures, for instance, generally contained an abundance of title cards to present on-screen that dialog which, at the time, could not be rendered as audible points of "the collocation devised".[197] These films also made large use of narrative title cards and exaggerated facial and bodily movements, so as to represent on-screen that emotional or other information which the film makers could not always depend upon being delivered musically, as "live" or independently recorded audible points of the collocation.[198]

With the advent of sound-on-film motion pictures, "the collocation devisable" by the motion picture "author" assumed a wider practical potential. Certain purely visual techniques all but disappeared, as much of the idea expression of the motion picture art was shifted to audible carriage in the motion picture soundtrack, there to operate and take substantive meaning in integrated association with the visual track.

Yet that a motion picture of 1920 might be deemed intelligible when considered as to its visual narrative does not mean that a motion picture of 1930 may have its intelligibility weighed only as to its visual track, or that we may apply such a copyrightability test to its isolated soundtrack also. The motion picture of 1930 represents a "species", but the motion picture of 1920 represents a "genus". While the copyrightability of the 1920 motion picture remains a matter of statutory recognition, the copyrightability of the 1930 motion picture is a matter of reasonable construction of the reach of that statutory recognition.

Further, the "species" may be distinguished from the "genus" because the "species" represents a shift in the "author's" manner of structuring "the collocation devised". This shift has been made by virtue of a

---

[197] The preclusion worked in the practical sense: technical possibilities were overridden by the realistic necessities attending the distribution of hundreds of prints of each film to thousands of movie theaters. In this market context, dialog-on-records could not meet required levels of amplification, bulk weight transport, prevention of wear, security from breakage, synchronization, etc. *See* note 88 *supra* and accompanying text.

[198] The insurance was again a practical one: while the movies always had music, the film producers were unable to exercise artistic control over the music provided their films until the soundtrack appeared. Thus, while pre-soundtrack film music could be very functional in limited respects, it was never as multi-dimensional in its linguistic functions as post-soundtrack film music. *See* note 94 *supra* and text accompanying notes 93-94 *supra*.

means which technologically did not attend the "author's" structuring of "the collocation devised" for carriage by the antecedent "genus". Yet the "species" is not a protectible outgrowth of the "genus" at all unless, like the "genus", it is a "writing". If, as with the "genus", it is "the collocation devised" for carriage by the "species" which a copyright shall protect if it may be conferred, then it is "the collocation devised" to which the tests of copyrightability must be applied. Any other procedural application of those tests could negate the benefit of the copyright recognition extended to the "genus", for the antecedent "genus" may be then or eventaully represented only to the extent its "species" is produced. That negation—perhaps even the threat of that negation—violates both the congressional grant and the promotive/protective constitutional charge underlying recognition of the antecedent "genus" as a "writing". Such violations simply may not pass where reason stands watch.

The tenability of these principles becomes especially clear when we consider the unreasonableness of applying the intelligibility and visual appreciability tests in contradiction to the procedure urged here as legal. Reference was made earlier to the idea expressions contained within certain segments of the film "Citizen Kane". We have seen, for example, that at one point of this film part of "the collocation devised" by the "author" concerns a structural identification of "Rosebud". During the scene in which this structural identification is made, the isolated visual track shows a young boy playing with a sled in the snow. The isolated dialog tracks for this scene carry the voice of a woman calling the name "Charles" in the foreground, and they also carry the sounds of a child's playful cries in the background. The isolated music tracks for this scene carry a musical narrative in which the "Rosebud" leitmotif is lyrically proclaimed. The isolated visual track may be visually appreciable, but it is not intelligible vis-à-vis the idea expression of the motion picture. All that the isolated visual track can say is: here is a young boy playing with a sled in the snow. The isolated soundtrack is not visually appreciable, nor is it intelligible via-à-vis the idea expression of the motion picture. All that the isolated soundtrack can say is that which the dialog tracks and music tracks say: the name "Charles" is being called to a happy child, and "Rosebud" is germane to this moment in his life. Only when "the collocation devised" of visible and audible points is considered as an entirety do we have the idea expression of the "author", as well as the visual appreciability and intelligibility of that idea expression. Only then does the application of these copyrightability tests make any sense as concerns protection of "the collocation devised" by the "author". Only then can we read: a young boy is playing with a sled in the snow; this young boy is "Charles" Foster Kane, and he is happy at this moment; and the physical identity and philosophical significance of "Rosebud" are rooted in this scene.

It may be noted that there is nothing unreasonable about the notion that we are *reading* these motion picture messages, even though these messages are delivered by use of audible points of reference as well as visible ones. What is involved is the physiological/psychological/aesthetic concept known as *synesthesia;* this refers to the sensation or image of a sense (as of color) other than the one (as of sound) being stimulated.[199] In the case of a sound-on-film motion picture, the manner in which cinematic phenomena are perceived is often grounded in this concept as applied. Viewers may attribute to the motion picture visual track effects that are owing primarily to elements incorporated on the soundtrack, or listeners may attribute to the motion picture soundtrack effects that are owing primarily to manipulation of the visual track. But the end of concurrent perception becomes, in fact or as potential, reception of the idea expression of—"the collocation devised" by—the motion picture "author".[200]

One need not push the implications of synesthesia so far as to encounter conceptual problems with certain mechanical recordings themselves. Where the sound-on-film motion picture is concerned, a visual coordinate is obviously present. In this context, the function of an aural coordinate is to bring the scope of the visual in line with the scope of the authorship which inheres in a motion picture work. A visual coordinate of **idea expression being present,** it therefore should be enough to satisfy a visual appreciability requisite of copyrightability.

---

[199] Anderson, *The Invisible Music,* STEREO REVIEW, Sept., 1974, at 4. Note that the concept of synesthesia has been posited by some writers as a justification for denying the viability of film music as "music" when film music is recorded or performed in concert so as to be enjoyed apart from its functions in motion pictures. *E.g., id.*

[200] Directors and composers experienced in working with this phenomenon have attempted to explain it in simple terms. William Walton calls the film composer "the servant of the eye" and notes that "music offers orchestral 'color' to the mind's ear in such a way that at every stage it confirms and reinforces the color on the screen which is engaging the eye." Walton, *Music For Shakespearean Films,* in FILM MUSIC 128, 130 (J. Limbacher ed. 1974). George Antheil called film music "a public communication" and noted: "You *see* love, and you *hear* it. Simultaneously. It makes sense. Music becomes a language for you, without your knowing it." THOMAS, *supra* note 151, at 171, *quoting* G. Antheil (emphasis in original). Sergei Eisenstein, the father of all film theoreticians, attempted to explain the music in his films as "no mere imprint of phenomena but their piercing light expressed in rays of sound." Eisenstein, *PRKFV,* in FILM MUSIC 159, 162 (J. Limbacher ed. 1974). Bronislau Kaper offers an apt analogy: "At certain moments in films, nobody knows the difference between what is visual and what is acoustical. It all comes together. It's like seeing and hearing lightning—it's one effect." THOMAS, *supra* note 151, at 90, *quoting* B. Kaper.

There would seem, then, to be nothing disturbing about employing intelligibility and visual appreciability tests in strict accord with the constitutional essence of copyrightability itself. Indeed, such use appears to be functionally ordained by the "reasonableness" maxim which inheres in "species of the genus" copyrightability analysis, and which operates to safeguard certain constitutional proprieties in that analysis. Moreover, such use has been sanctioned even where only aesthetic logic, rather than something as weighty as constitutionally charted logic, has been perceived as the analytical impetus.

Reference was made earlier to the protection extended to motion pictures as "cinematographic works" under the Universal Copyright Convention. That protection was seen to embrace motion picture soundtracks. However, the isolated motion picture soundtrack is incapable of being visually perceived as to its underlying works; and works must be capable of visual perception to be published and protected under the Convention.[201] The motion picture soundtrack and the visual perception requirement of the Convention have been harmonized, within that non-judicial context, simply by directing to the sound-on-film motion picture the analytical attention which its aesthetic distinctions demand. The commentary by Bogsch on this issue first defines a "cinematographic work" as "the sum total of different arts" which "are amalgamated in a unified whole and incorporated by the cinematographic film."[202] Then it notes:

> ...there is a possibility that the words "read or otherwise visually perceived" may lead to misunderstanding if applied to cinematographic works. A cinematographic work is perceived both visually and by the ear, at least if it is a sound film, as the overwhelming majority of modern cinematographic works are. There is no doubt that the negative and positive films (comprising both picture band and sound track) are copies of the cinematographic work; and that if these copies are generally distributed to the public, for example, by selling thousands of copies, the cinematographic work will be published. However, it may be argued that not any copy can cause publication but only copies serving visual perception; that sound films serve not only visual perception but also perception by the ear. There may be some merit in this argument. However, sound

---

[201] Article VI of the Universal Copyright Convention reads:
'Publication', as used in this Convention, means the reproduction in tangible form and the general distribution to the public of copies of a work from which it can be read or otherwise visually perceived.
[202] A. Bogsch, The Law of Copyright Under the Universal Convention 71 (1964).

films are also intended for visual perception. Once this element is present, it satisfies the words "read or otherwise visually perceived" of Article VI.[203]

Neither the logic of the analysis nor the justice of the result is undercut by any legislative action or administrative procedure noted earlier as regards treatment of the motion picture soundtrack. Indeed, the attitude of the House Judiciary Committee on soundtrack protection, identified in the Committee's report on the Sound Recording Act and effectuated by action of the Copyright Office, is supported by this analysis.[204]

As noted earlier, the Copyright Office's practice of refusing to register an isolated motion picture soundtrack, or a soundtrack offered as the only new matter in a previously published or registered motion picture, has been urged in anti-protectionist theory as authority for denying the copyrightability of all motion picture soundtracks.[205] However, nothing even remotely suggestive of such authority need be read in this practice. A lone soundtrack, bearing sounds which are not integrally conjoined with photographic images, is neither visually appreciable nor intelligible vis-à-vis the collocated idea expression of a motion picture "author". Its rejection is a logical mandate of the very approach under which it is protectible as an integrated part of a motion picture when offered for registration as such.

---

[203] *Id.* at 73-74.
[204] The Committee's attitude is reflected in the text accompanying note 37 *supra* and in the following continuance thereof, at 117 CONG. REC. 1566, 1571 (1971):

> Under the existing title 17, "motion pictures" represent a broad genus whose fundamental characteristic is a series of related images that impart an impression of motion when shown in succession, including any sounds integrally conjoined with the images. Under this concept the physical form in which the motion picture is fixed—film, tape, discs, and so forth—is irrelevant, and the same is true whether the images reproduced in the physical object can be made out with the naked eye or require optical, electronic, or other special equipment to be perceived.

Note that no mitigation of this attitude inheres in the proposed Copyright Revision Bill, S. 1361, 93d Cong., 1st Sess. (1973). Motion pictures are identified in the proposed legislation as a sub-class of "audio visual works" and are defined thus, *id.* §101:

> "Motion pictures" are audiovisual works consisting of a series of related images which, when shown in succession, impart an impression of motion, together with accompanying sounds, if any.

[205] *See* note 68 *supra* and accompanying text.

The logic which mandates rejection of a soundtrack offered as the only new matter in a previously published or registered motion picture is almost identical. The added difference in this instance is that the motion picture proprietor has earlier made his bargain with the public by publishing or registering the motion picture without inclusion of the later proffered soundtrack. The examples provided by the Copyright Office in this regard are illustrative of how that bargain can be made without also jeopardizing the copyrightability of the motion picture itself, though it be considered independent from the later proffered soundtrack for purpose of *White-Smith* analysis. "An old silent picture with a new soundtrack"[206] bears "the collocation devised" by its "author" without attachment of the new soundtrack, because "the collocation devised" was structured at a time when certain visual techniques, now antiquated, could be utilized to posit elements of the collocation which today would be structured aurally. "A previously published foreign film with a dubbed soundtrack in English"[207] bears "the collocation devised" by its "author" without attachment of a dubbed soundtrack in English, because "the collocation devised" was originally structured by inclusion of a foreign language soundtrack. Just as the motion picture soundtrack is protectible as part of an integrated motion picture when offered for registration as such, these Copyright Office examples are protectible while their later included soundtracks are not protectible under a *White-Smith* analysis which neither violates the analytical strictures of *White-Smith* nor the copyrightability concerns of the Constitution.

If anything further need be said of *White-Smith* germane to the soundtrack copyrightability issue, it is this. While *White-Smith* may appear superficially to be the most threatening of explosives set by anti-protectionist theorists under the wings of a protectionist rationale, the case emerges substantively as the most devastating of legal mines which discharge their conceptual loads in the face of anti-protectionist theory itself. More than reason determines such a result, for intelligibility and visual appreciability tests are copyrightability tests. Copyrightability tests exist to examine amenability to a statutory charter in which inheres a special kind of constitutionality. *White-Smith* cannot be applied to resolve a copyrightability question in a manner which deems constitutionality of no or merely piecemeal relevance. Nor need *White-Smith*, properly understood, be in any way ignored. In the context of an applied "species of the genus" copyrightability analysis, *White-Smith* may be deemed useful as an analytical tool when wedded to a reason which preserves constitutional

---

[206] *See* Example 1 in note 68 *supra*.
[207] *See* Example 2 in note 68 *supra*.

propriety. The substance of its rules and the sense of their utility derive from an aesthetic constitutional definition and a promotive/protective constitutional charge, and these the courts have consistently approached in reasonable fashion when applying "species of the genus" doctrine to a copyrightability issue. Thus, *White-Smith* emerges as no less than a structural support of protectionist rationale itself. Failing as an arm in the arsenal of anti-protectionist thought, it may be identified not only as leaving that arsenal, but as leaving that arsenal empty.

Unfortunately, the absence of logical and legal support does not leave that arsenal without societal meaning. The promotion of anti-protectionist theory is recent, yet its history may be measured in years. The attack on motion picture property during the 1970s has involved a purely intellectual assault on motion picture copyright, but it has embraced as well the drawing of economic blood. No analysis of the former would be complete or even practical without investigation of the latter, given its continuing presence and projected growth. We pass, then, from an analytical consideration of intellectual mischief to a confrontation with crime—an element which has accorded anti-protectionist theory its most unctuous approval.

III. *MOTION PICTURE SOUNDTRACK PIRACY*

(A) The Economics of Soundtrack Piracy

Organized soundtrack piracy did not even exist in the United States until the very beginning of 1973. Upon arrival, its practice evidenced a marketing insight and an operational style which left the rampant jazz piracy of the early 1950s looking like the invention of amateurs.[208]

In January of 1973, the first record piracy operation wholly devoted to the marketing of appropriated motion picture soundtracks entered the United States record market. Its organizers billed the company as "Cinema Records". "Cinema's" marketing activities were relatively unconcealed,[209] and its commercial success was instantaneous. The outfit was immediately followed into the soundtrack piracy business by "Sound/Stage Recordings". "Cinema" and "Sound/Stage" operated from

---

[208] *See Piracy on Records,* 5 STAN. L. REV. 433 (1953).

[209] The organization's product packaging did, however, attribute performances of the pirated/bootlegged soundtrack material to a fictitious orchestra. Other "throw-off" devices employed by soundtrack piracy organizations are "Recorded in Europe" tags, phony conductor credits, "Not for Profit" disclaimers, and even copying prohibition warnings.

bases in California, but their products reached record retail outlets throughout the nation. Neither organization encountered any legal resistance from federal or state anti-piracy authorities. Both organizations, however, were carefully watched by would-be record pirates, bootleggers, and counterfeiters savoring the small fortunes being made by the soundtrack raiders. When it was apparent by mid-1973 that "Cinema" and "Sound/Stage", for whatever reason, had incurred not opposition but rather a de facto license to loot, the would-be's became active coast to coast. In the ensuing two years, some two dozen soundtrack piracy operations have taken the domestic field.

The new record piracy—new in the sense that its objective was virgin, its de facto immunity was unprecedented, and its generally open marketing procedure was unheard of—is essentially an illicit economic response to two developments. The first and earlier of these was the appearance in the United States of what has been identified as the soundtrack market.[210] The second was the recognition and demonstration, by legitimate record companies, of the large profit opportunities inhering in that market.

As to the former, it may be defined as a sub-market within the market for records, itself quite vast. Consumers within the soundtrack market purchase soundtrack albums of musical significance. These are records of original, serious musical scores or scoring excerpts from motion pictures. Many soundtrack consumers are soundtrack collectors—persons who have acquired or who intend to acquire hundreds of film music records and whose hobby it is to acquire virtually all important film music records which exist.

The soundtrack market finds its origin in the practice of record companies and/or film companies to release soundtrack albums concurrently with the release of source films. For the past thirty years, such albums have been manufactured and marketed at an approximate retail price of $5. Though such releases now number in the thousands, they have always been very few relative to the number of original film scores composed each year. Generally, these albums remained "in print" so long as the source films remained in theatrical release. Unless such albums became surprise money makers, they went "out of print" when their source films were withdrawn from release. With production of the individual albums halted in this manner, the albums themselves became rare records as retail stores sold out or returned their stock.

The appetite for such albums remained intact with the passage of years, however. By the beginning of the 1970s, demand for the old, out of

---

[210] Sutak, *The Investment Market in Movie Music Albums,* HIGH FIDELITY, July, 1972, at 62.

print soundtrack album releases was intensive enough to establish market prices for the rare records which begin at the $20-$25-$30 range, average out at the $40-$50-$60 range, start to tip at the $100-$150-$200 range, and in exceptional cases peak at the $1000-$1500-$2000 range.[211]

One journalist has attempted to define the rationale of this phenomenon. His research question was economic; his answer was aesthetic as well:

> Why these prices, and who is paying them? The *why* is attributed to the current demand-versus-supply factor—original press runs were minimal and those not sold were scrapped and melted down, leaving an inventory of zero. The *who* is a market not existing ten and twenty years ago—the young students and film enthusiasts of today, who are more knowledgeable and appreciative of the history of film scoring, an art which they contend to be the only innovative musical medium of this century.[212]

The direction of this film music demand is linked with a history of film music composition. As we have seen, the forms of film music composition were relatively established by the early 1930s. Thereafter, the contributions of "old masters" like Max Steiner, Erich Korngold, Alfred Newman, Dimitri Tiomkin, Franz Waxman, Victor Young, Bronislau Kaper, David Raksin, Hugo Friedhofer, Miklos Rozsa, and Bernard Herrmann, together with the works of "new wave" composers like Alex North, Elmer Bernstein, Leonard Rosenman, Andre Pevin, Ernest Gold, Jerome Moross, Henry Mancini, and Jerry Goldsmith, created a "Golden Age of Film Scoring" in American films, the effects of which may still be felt in the better-made films of today.

It was the out of print recorded music of composers such as these which ran rare soundtrack album prices up to astonishing levels by the beginning of the 1970s. The legitimate record companies were hardly unmoved by news that items such as $50 or $1500 records existed, especially since such prices continued to climb. Yet convinced as they were about the intensity of this demand, the decision makers at these companies were quite skeptical about the extent of this demand. However, the waters of the vintage film music phenomenon did seem worthy of an

---

[211] The market price record is currently held by the RCA LP of Max Steiner's score for "The Caine Mutiny" ('54) (currently over $2,000 per copy). Runners-up include the GE LP of Bernard Herrmann's television opera "A Child Is Born" ('55) and the Ford LP of Alex North's score for "American Road" ('53) (both currently about $1,500 per copy).

[212] Considine, *Soundtracks: Bon-Bons, Yip-ee-i-o's...*, N.Y. Times, Aug. 27, 1972, §D, at 20, col. 1.

experimental dip, and one was taken. It was entitled "The Sea Hawk: The Classic Film Scores of Erich Wolfgang Korngold", an album produced by RCA featuring newly recorded excerpts from several film scores composed by a deceased musician whose deification had remained a matter of musical controversy for more than half a century. The disc was released shortly before Christmas of 1972. By that Christmas, the record was the largest selling classical recording of 1972; today it is almost the largest selling classical record of all time. And: after "The Sea Hawk" came the deluge.

It has been two years since the renaissance began, and in that time the world of serious musical recordings has shifted mightily. The best sellers of that changed world have not been performances of Tchaikovsky, Brahms, or Beethoven, but rather performances of vintage Korngold, Steiner, Newman, Rozsa, Waxman, and Herrmann. Recordings of vintage Tiomkin, Friedhofer, Raksin, Kaper, and Young are slated for future market success. Film music societies have been formed to issue recordings of full scores, these produced either through the independent rerecording of old scores or by the independent licensing of soundtrack recording rights in newer scores. Film music works by the "old masters" are being joined with those of the second generation "new wavers" in invariably sold out concerts held in cities as diverse as Hollywood, Buffalo, and London. Symphonies, concertos, cantatas, and chamber works by the same composers are being released by record companies. Walton, Vaughan-Williams, Bliss, Copland, Antheil, Thomson, Prokoviev, and Shostakovich are being discovered by youngsters weened on rock music and movie music, simply because these classicists have written some of the finest of all movie music. A half-dozen major record companies have embarked on reissue programs, returning many repackaged soundtrack recordings of the 1950s to the current marketplace. Most importantly, film producers, many of whom sent movies and movie music spiraling into a decade-long artistic depression by insisting on "pop song" scoring in recent years, have reacted to the huge box-office success of recent seriously scored films by perceiving anew that movies are less than moving when their soundtracks are aesthetically defective.[213]

If the renaissance is multi-leveled, its only negative aspect is the proliferation of soundtrack piracy. This development is particularly unsettling, for the motion picture industry is beset by many more internal problems than one which has, until recently, affected only record man-

---

[213] *See* Bernstein, *supra* note 85; Raksin, *Whatever Became of Movie Music?*, FILMMUSIC NOTEBOOK, Autumn, 1974, at 22.

ufacturers and performers.[214] In two years, over one hundred vintage motion pictures have had their soundtracks fall prey to piracy, and the economic loss represented by the appropriation is not inconsiderable.[215]

More importantly, the two year tally appears to represent only the beginning of the robbery. New soundtrack piracy organizations appear almost monthly. Solicitations appear regularly in soundtrack market literature, seeking to tap any and all sources, in the film industry or out, that can supply vintage film music tracks for eventual delivery in the marketplace. Certain well known repositories of such materials

---

[214] Most seriously, there is the problem of *film* piracy, which has grown rapidly in recent years and now costs the motion picture industry an estimated $50,000,000 to $100,000,000 in lost revenues each year. The rapid growth of film piracy is largely attributable to the motion picture industry's past attempts to ignore piracy out of existence. However, the need for a coordinated industry-wide attack on film piracy was recognized in 1974, and on Feb. 19, 1975, the Motion Picture Industry Association of America disclosed plans to establish a security organization (now the MPAA Print Security Office) to combat film piracy. The MPAA organization operates as the "prime instrument in locating pirates, and cooperating with the police authorities and prosecutors' office in putting these pirates in jail." *World-Wide War on Pix Print Pirates*, Variety, Feb. 19, 1975, at 5, col. 3. *quoting* J. Valenti, MPAA president. In one sense, film piracy may be regarded as subsuming soundtrack piracy, since film pirates duplicate film soundtracks as well as film visual tracks when they duplicate motion pictures. However, the film piracy network and the soundtrack piracy network are otherwise quite distinct in their marketing operations, such that the soundtrack piracy network has remained unscathed throughout the present war on film piracy as well as throughout the continuing war on record piracy. To date, a number of criminal indictments, both state and federal, have been returned against various film piracy organizations, but no indictments, either state or federal, have been returned against soundtrack piracy organizations. The de facto immunity of the soundtrack piracy network from state and federal criminal laws has operated despite the fact that the various film pirates presently under criminal indictment are charged, in part, with violation of the same criminal laws which are violated by soundtrack piracy organizations. *See: Id.*; *Suspect in Piracy of Films is Seized*, N.Y. Times, Feb. 20, 1975, at 40, col. 1; *Raid On Print Pirate; Title Range Shock*, Variety, Feb. 26, 1975, at 28, col. 1; Movie Bootlegger Suspect Seized, N.Y. Post, Feb. 20, 1975, at 40, col. 1.

[215] Base fees paid for licenses to record motion picture music tracks range from $5,000 to $10,000 per source film, plus a percentage of net profits earned by the record manufacturer. Thus, the revenue loss to the motion picture industry represented by the current tally of appropriated soundtracks is probably over $1,000,000. This loss appears relatively slight when contrasted with annual lost revenues caused by film piracy. *See* note 214 *supra*. It is important to note, however, that annual lost revenues caused by film piracy have reached greater amounts only because film piracy drew no organized opposition when film piracy first appeared on an organized basis.

—university libraries which have been storing film scores and music tracks donated by composers and film companies for the purpose of making these available to film and music scholars now and in the future—have been forced to cancel general accessibility to much of their research collections as a result.[216]

Yet the universities have been alone in their activated response to organized soundtrack piracy. Legitimate record companies, which in many cases are licensees of the right to record the music tracks now being pirated, have not acted because their predominant anti-piracy concern is with appropriation of current product.[217] Film composers have not acted because, almost without exception, they have no standing to act.[218] Federal and state criminal authorities have not acted for reasons which will become evident when we consider the operation and legal status of soundtrack piracy. Independent of some confusing legal implications, the soundtrack piracy situation has become so frustrating to some of the interests being harmed that one famous composer is reported to have attacked, with swinging cane in hand, a shelf full of pirated soundtrack albums containing his music in a New York City record shop.[219]

The problem of soundtrack piracy cannot, of course, be settled by waving a cane in vehement assault upon recordings which either are or are not stolen goods provided by persons who either are or are not criminals. But the problem can be settled. And if the settlement lies beyond the beclouding of the issue which has occurred in the theorizing of the law, it also lies beyond the confusions which cling to the enforcement of the law.

B. *The Operation of Soundtrack Piracy*

Most of the domestic soundtrack piracy outfits operate from California. However, the largest of all such organizations—"Curtain Calls Records"—operates from a base in New York. Given what is perceived to be an immunity produced by legal confusion and litigative inconvenience, few soundtrack piracy operatives make any attempt to cloak their activities. The distribution channels through which their products pass to consumers are multiple, and the most important of these channels is even

---

[216] The major university film music libraries are located at Syracuse University (The George Arents Research Library) and at the University of Wyoming (The Division of Rare Books and Special Collections).
[217] This explanation was uniformly offered—on a not-for-attribution basis—by representatives of record companies queried by the author.
[218] *See* Lees, *When the Music Stopped*, HIGH FIDELITY, July, 1972, at 20.
[219] *Pirates*, PRO MUSICA SANA, Summer, 1974, at 16.

unique. So, too, is a specialized financing arrangement often employed by soundtrack pirates to generate the income which makes large scale soundtrack piracy immediately profitable.

Like other forms of record piracy, soundtrack piracy embraces three distinct methods of stealing sound: piracy, bootlegging, and counterfeiting. The soundtrack pirate engages in piracy *per se* when he duplicates a legitimate recording and then sells the pirated disc under a pirate label and in pirate packaging. The soundtrack pirate engages in bootlegging when, without a license, he transfers the never-before-recorded music tracks of a film to records which are then made available for sale. Occasionally, the source of such booty is not a film soundtrack but rather a tape of a radio broadcast of concertised film music. The soundtrack counterfeiter, as he operates within the context of organized soundtrack piracy, duplicates the recording, the label, and the packaging of the bogus product produced by his pirate/bootlegger competitor.

Unlike the practices which characterize record piracy in general, the piracy and counterfeiting which inhere in organized soundtrack piracy are never directed toward duplication of currently available legitimate recordings. The legitimate records duplicated by soundtrack pirates are invariably out of print, rare soundtrack albums which sell for extremely high prices as legitimate issues. This type of piracy is highly profitable because a pirate edition of a legitimate album which sells for $100 per copy can be sold for anywhere from $5 to $25. Similarly, the soundtrack pirate's style of counterfeiting is highly profitable because, by adopting a credo of dishonor among thieves, a competitor who manufactures and sells pirate or bootleg soundtrack albums can be undercut in price when *his* efforts are appropriated. Soundtrack piracy may also be distinguished from generic record piracy in that soundtrack pirates deal more in the manufacture and sale of records than in the manufacture and sale of tapes.

One other feature of the soundtrack pirate's product invites close attention: it sometimes may be defined in terms of an eclectic illegality.

For reasons owing to concern with technical sound quality,[220] soundtrack albums issued by legitimate record companies do not always contain the same recording of the motion picture score as was used in the source film itself. Sometimes these albums contain a rerecording of the score—a recording made independently of that made for the film soundtrack, though the same personnel may be employed to produce both. Sometimes these albums contain a mixture of rerecorded excerpts from the

---

[220] *See* Margolis, *Why Soundtrack Albums Don't Sound Better,* HIGH FIDELITY, July, 1972, at 59.

score and excerpts taken directly from the film soundtrack. Even where the legitimate soundtrack album contains material taken exclusively from the film soundtrack by direct transfer, the disc often omits other musical material contained on the film soundtrack. The omitted material may often exist, as a rerecorded excerpt (especially in the case of songs) or as a direct soundtrack quotation, on *another* legitimate record album.

Thus, in compiling musical material to produce a bogus soundtrack album, the soundtrack pirate often has a range of material from which to draw. He may produce an album which contains only the duplication of a legitimate soundtrack album, and this bogus product may be (1) a duplication of an original, direct transfer soundtrack album, (2) a duplication of a soundtrack album containing a rerecorded score, or (3) a duplication of a soundtrack album which mixes direct transfer soundtrack quotations with rerecorded excerpts from the score. To his duplication of an original, direct transfer soundtrack album, he may add the duplication of a recorded song, from the same score, which appeared originally in rerecorded form on another legitimate album. Similarly, to his duplication of a soundtrack album containing a rerecorded score, he may add recorded excerpts from the same score taken directly from the film soundtrack. He may even offer excerpts from two or more film scores in one bogus package, some taken directly from film soundtracks (or from legitimate soundtrack albums which contain direct transfer quotations), the rest taken from legitimate rerecordings of film music materials.

Thus, in many instances the soundtrack pirate's product represents a combination pirate/bootleg soundtrack album. And counterfeit product produced by soundtrack pirates represent combination counterfeit/pirate soundtrack albums, combination counterfeit/bootleg soundtrack albums, or combination counterfeit/pirate/bootleg soundtrack albums.

As will be seen, these distinctions become crucial when the issue of the legal culpability of soundtrack pirates arises. Our present consideration, however, mandates attention to the interesting manner by which the fruits of soundtrack piracy are served to their consumers.

Just as the "demand" side of the domestic soundtrack market exhibits unique economic characteristics relative to pricing, the "supply" side of this market evidences certain marketing attributes not shared by more common record distribution networks. As was suggested earlier, the recognition of a widespread consumer demand for serious film music recordings occurred at three levels and at three times. Initially, this demand was recognized and attended to "informally" during the mid-1960s by small scale entrepreneurs. Later, when the great success of the "informal" marketers began to generate magazine and newspaper reports during the early 1970s, the "formal" record companies recognized this demand and proceeded to tap it in earnest. Finally, the reported success of the "informal" marketers, the more obvious success of the "formal" marketers, and the sudden legal confusion stirred by antiprotectionist claims in the area of motion picture soundtrack protection, encouraged record pirates, bootleggers, and counterfeiters to enter the soundtrack market, where they have remained and where more continue to migrate at great profit, while carving a truly different form of record piracy out of the generic record piracy pie.

The supply network of prime concern in this analysis derives from the growth of those responsible for the first instance of demand recognition: the small scale entrepreneurs, who are no longer so small in terms of their market importance. Originally, these market actors operated solely from retail record stores located in large cities like New York and Los Angeles. Perceiving a new, high price demand for out of print soundtrack albums in the mid-1960s, these retailers conducted or authorized wide-ranging supply hunts throughout the nation. At the same time, they converted portions of their stores into rare soundtrack album repositories. Within time, they gained reputations as high priced soundtrack album specialists.

Their activities were watched closely by other small entrepreneurs, who quickly concluded that the high price demand for old soundtrack albums was geographically broad and, hence, could be tapped by mail. Like the record store retailers-turned-soundtrack specialists, the mail-order marketers traveled from town to town, city to city, and state to state buying up old soundtrack album stock found in out-of-the-way record shops, discount record bins, and flea markets. Like some of the record store retailers themselves, the mail-order salesmen published catalogs listing their large inventories and high prices, advertised in music and film magazines, and both collected their money and distributed their wares through mail-order operations.

Today, and together, the mail-order soundtrack dealers and the record store soundtrack specialists manage to blanket the United States and foreign countries in terms of tapping demand for the old soundtrack albums at their new prices. Most of the business done in this market goes to approximately a dozen dealerships, evenly divided as to both mail-order/record store type and West Coast/East Coast location. While the record store retailer type of dealership is the most visible of these marketing systems, the mail-order seller type of dealership looms as the most important. For the mail-order dealers' catalog and brochure publications bind many thousands of interested consumers, located in all states and in several countries, to a handful of major distribution centers. The mail-order dealers themselves usually possess resale and occupancy licenses issued by their respective states, their organizations are each staffed with several employees, and their operations are entirely legitimate with one possible exception: the mail-order dealers provide the primary means utilized by soundtrack piracy organizations for the sale of pirated, bootlegged, and counterfeited soundtrack albums to thousands of consumers.

This was much less the almost uniform case which exists today when the soundtrack piracy outfits made their market debut early in 1973. When "Cinema Records" and "Sound/Stage Recordings" began to issue large quantities of pirate and bootleg soundtrack discs from California, and as "Curtain Calls Records" appeared shortly afterward in New York to offer both a large catalog of high priced bootleg soundtrack albums and an integrated mail-order system to handle national distribution, the feeling was widespread among legitimate soundtrack sellers that "Cinema", "Sound/Stage", and "Curtain Calls" could not appropriate so many motion picture music tracks and record company soundtrack albums, or make so much money from the appropriations, or operate so brazenly, without incurring a legal reckoning. Thus, the wares pushed by these organizations were handled very sparingly at first by mail-order dealers.

Yet not only did the trio of soundtrack piracy pathfinders remain legally unopposed, the three organizations so flaunted their perceived immunity that within six months of their appearance, "Curtain Calls" had achieved a roaring nationwide mail-order success while "Cinema" and "Sound/Stage" had won nationwide distribution through legitimate wholesalers supplying key retail outlets throughout the country. This half-year period of sustained motion picture soundtrack looting, attended by a de facto license to loot, ended all hesitation on the part of major soundtrack marketers. Soundtrack piracy organizations were then swiftly and almost universally embraced by the mail-order distributors as key suppliers, and a score of new soundtrack piracy organizations rose east and west to join "Cinema", "Sound/Stage", and "Curtain Calls" on the front lines of the great motion picture soundtrack robbery.

The embrace of soundtrack piracy by the soundtrack market's major actors also marked a vital shift in the financial arrangements which attend the manufacture and distribution of pirate, bootleg, and counterfeit records within this market. For with distribution through the mail-order organizations came direct contact with an international market of inveterate soundtrack collectors, film music addicts, and old fashioned suckers. Given that breakthrough, and with a burgeoning profit outlook and a perceived practical immunity to spur them on, the soundtrack piracy organizations next introduced a game plan for motion picture soundtrack appropriation which was not to be surpassed in its financial allurement by any gambit yet devised within the world of record piracy. No longer, it was seen, need soundtrack piracy organizations manufacture bogus soundtrack albums and *then* invade the marketplace with their product. Now, instead, the musical chairs of manufacture and sale could be switched: the market itself could be used to finance the movie music depredation *in advance.*

That is to say, the soundtrack piracy organizations could now inform the mail-order soundtrack dealers of pirate and/or bootleg soundtrack albums *to be produced.* The dealers, in turn, could announce the news of the upcoming productions to thousands of consumers through promotions inserted in the internationally distributed periodic sales letters and brochures published by the dealers. Though the present unavailability of the bogus soundtrack albums would have to be conceded, consumers could be invited to mail in their payments for the discs *immediately.* Indeed, consumers could be urged to place their "reservations" quickly, perhaps at special "pre-release prices", for records which "might" become available in "very limited quantities" at some time in the near future ("If enough response is generated you will receive your record in April"). The dealer-solicitor generally could deny guaranteed delivery of the soundtrack spoils "except to reserve order customers". To hopefully protect from possible implication in an illegal enterprise, the mail-order dealer could even tell his customers something like: "The legal staff of the manufacturer stated that this recording does not violate U. S. copyright requirements."[221]

Thereafter, payments from hundreds to thousands of customers desiring the bogus disc would flow through the mails to the mail-order distributors. A certain amount of the receipts would be channeled back to the "independent label" manufacturer. The manufacturer would take his immediate profit out of his receipts. The rest of the money would be used to make robbery a reality.

If the procedure appeared initially to be a record pirate's fantasy, it nevertheless worked wonderfully in fact. "Foreign American Productions" led the way with bravado, announcing an intention "if enough response is generated" to begin a large scale piracy operation by which various motion picture soundtrack recordings would be lifted off of their foreign release labels to be made available in the United States at $8 per pirated disc.[222] Other soundtrack piracy organizations quickly adopted the consortium technique of record piracy. Soon the soundtrack market mail-order exchange system was awash in announcements of upcoming

---

[221] *Special Pressing Advance Notice* 1 (Promotion distributed by Sound Track Album Retailers, Winter, 1974).
[222] *Id.* at 1-2.

appropriations and invitations urging the placement of "reservations" at "pre-release prices", these distinguishing an unprecedented system of manufacture and distribution in the world of record piracy. The system has, in fact, bequeathed the worst of all possible record piracy worlds: one in which pirate and bootleg recordings are conceived in union with the public, nursed in disregard of any applicable law with the participation of otherwise legitimate distributors, and delivered—after the fact of profit—first through the mails and then also through nationwide retail stores serviced by otherwise legitimate wholesalers.

It is this consortium system of soundtrack piracy, together with the integrated form of piracy whereby a manufacturer wields its own mail-order distribution network, which operate and flourish in the United States today. Announcements of projected soundtrack appropriations appear in soundtrack market literature at a rough average of two or three forthcoming production news breaks each month. Where soundtrack appropriations are made by an integrated manufacturer/distributor, brochures listing the organization's ever expanding catalog of soundtrack booty are advertised in national film and music magazines in classic record piracy fashion, supplying box addresses but mentioning no names other than that of the soundtrack piracy organization itself.

Such developments as these, however unfortunate, may have proved valuable in two respects. Organized soundtrack piracy, by dealing motion picture property the kind of sustained economic blows which generally would be legally permissible if the anti-protectionist claims we considered could be supported in law, has served to demonstrate the implicit end of anti-protectionist theory itself. At the same time, by delivering such blows irrespective of the protection accorded motion picture property by law, and pursuant to the perception that protection of property by law may be disregarded when prolonged non-application of law leaves the same property to be savaged, organized soundtrack piracy has served to demonstrate the harms which follow when protectionist laws go unenforced, whether because they are insisted to be groundless or because they present a small mire of procedural difficulties too frontally confusing to be faced.

As every vestige of anti-protectionist theory is seen to crumble analytically, the organized economic activity which bears a clearly illegal status once its theoretical sanction is discredited may be identified as necessitating the application of law. Still, if motion picture soundtrack protection is to be more than a meaningless notation imbedded in written copyright law, then the proceedings which give effect to such protection must be precisely reasoned, their pitfalls fully understood. Such requisites arise because, paradoxically, the soundtrack pirate and certain of his distributors stand as the most vulnerable and the most slippery of all criminal actors operating within the field of record piracy. Our final analysis will evidence why this is so, and why vulnerability remains singularly pronounced when the oils provided to the criminal actor by copyright law are understood and thereby dissolved.

(C) The Challenge of Soundtrack Piracy

As we have seen, no element of generic record piracy has enjoyed a freedom from legal interference comparable to that accorded to organized soundtrack piracy. How incongruous to note, then, that no element involved in organized record piracy is as ripe for plucking by law enforcement authorities, or as legally pluckable, as is organized soundtrack piracy. The explanation of so unique a paradox lies in the peculiar interrelationship of the copyright law of the United States, the anti-piracy laws of the several states, and the variant nature of the stolen beast itself—the illicit soundtrack recording.

The Copyright Act has long provided that certain infringements of copyright are not only civil violations but also criminal violations. Section 104(a) provides that any person who, for profit, willfully infringes a federal copyright shall be deemed guilty of a federal misdemeanor.[223] Punishment of such a person, upon conviction, is by imprisonment in federal prison lasting up to one year and/or by fine of up to $1000.[224] Moreover, the same criminal penalties apply to any person who knowingly and willfully aids or abets such an infringement.[225]

Prior to October 15, 1971, there was an express exception to this rule of criminal liability within the Copyright Act. This exception held that when a person, by the unauthorized manufacture, use, or sale of records or tapes, infringed a musical copyright held by a copyright owner who had given up his exclusive right to record under a compulsory license agreement, that infringer would not be subject to criminal liability.[226]

This exception was entirely deleted from the Copyright Act on October 15, 1971.[227] At the same time, it was superseded by one of the

---

[223] 17 U.S.C. §104 was recently amended by 88 Stat. 1873 (1974), Pub. L. 93-573. 17 U.S.C. §104(a), amending 17 U.S.C. §104 reads in appropriate part:

> Except as provided in subsection (b), any person who willfully and for profit shall infringe any copyright secured by this title, or who shall knowingly and willfully aid or abet such infringement, shall be deemed guilty of a misdemeanor, and upon conviction thereof shall be punished by imprisonment for not exceeding one year or by a fine of not less than $100 nor more than $1,000, or both, in the discretion of the court....

[224] 17 U.S.C. §104(a), *amending* 17 U.S.C. §104. *See also* note 230 *infra*.

[225] 17 U.S.C. §104(a), *amending* 17 U.S.C. §104. *See also* note 230 *infra*.

provisions of the Sound Recording Act.[228] The new provision became available to protect the owner of a musical copyright immediately—on October 15, 1971.

The balance of the sound recording amendment, providing for the copyrightability of records and tapes,[229] became effective on February 15, 1972. Thus, working in two directions within one legislative act, Congress brought record piracy itself within the terms of the federal copyright law providing for federal criminal penalties.[230] Hence, unauthorized duplication of copyrighted records and tapes is now a federal crime, and infringement of a musical copyright via the duplication of copyrighted *or* uncopyrighted records and tapes appears to be a federal crime as well.[231]

---

[226] Act of March 4, 1909, ch. 320, §25, 35 Stat. 1081, *as amended* 17 U.S.C. §101(e), read in appropriate part:

> Whenever the owner of a musical copyright has used or permitted the use of the copyrighted work upon the parts of musical instruments serving to reproduce mechanically the musical work, then in case of infringement of such copyright by the unauthorized manufacture, use, or sale of interchangeable parts, such as disks, rolls, bands, or cylinders for use in mechanical music-producing machines adapted to reproduce the copyrighted music, no criminal action shall be brought, but in a civil action an injunction may be granted upon such terms as the court may impose, and the plaintiff shall be entitled to recover in lieu of profits and damages a royalty. . . .

[227] Act of Oct. 15, 1971, 85 Stat. 391, Pub. L. 92-140 §2.

[228] *Id.*

[229] Act of Oct. 15, 1971, 85 Stat. 391, Pub. L. 92-140 §1.

[230] An expiration date contained in the Sound Recording Act has since been removed, and the criminal provisions of 17 U.S.C. §104 have since been expanded to increase the penalties covering unauthorized duplication of copyrighted sound recordings. 17 U.S.C. §104(b), *amending* 17 U.S.C. §104, reads:

> Any person who willfully and for profit shall infringe any copyright provided by section 1(f) of this title [providing for the copyrightability of sound recordings], or who shall knowingly and willfully aid or abet such infringement, shall be fined not more than $25,000 or imprisoned not more than one year, or both, for the first offense and shall be fined not more than $50,000 or imprisoned not more than two years, or both, for any subsequent offense.

[231] The issues of whether or not record pirates may be prosecuted and convicted under federal copyright law for a crime of *infringement of a musical copyright via unauthorized duplication,* and of where that leaves the constitutionality of state anti-piracy laws if they can, are believed to be beyond the scope of the present analysis. However, since approaching discussion focuses on the ability of the

Of these two crimes, that of unauthorized duplication has won prime attention in recent years, for the reason that sound recordings produced prior to the effective date of the Sound Recording Act's extension of copyright remain unprotected by the criminal sanctions of the federal copyright law which apply to copying *per se*. However, passage of the Sound Recording Act bore no effect on motion picture soundtrack protection as to location in time. As noted earlier, when Congress amended the copyright law on October 15, 1971, Congress excluded the film soundtrack from the net of criminal liability established by the Sound

---

state anti-piracy authorities as well as the ability of federal anti-piracy authorities to attack soundtrack piracy, some preliminary observations on the problems which spring from these issues may be made.

The issue of the viability of a crime of *infringement of a musical copyright via unauthorized duplication* arises for two reasons. For one, the provision of former law excepting record piracy from criminal liability for infringement of a musical copyright was deleted from the federal copyright law on Oct. 15, 1971, effective that date; this action implicates the existence of such a crime under federal law since that date. *See* notes 226-27 *supra* and text accompanying notes 226-28 *supra*. For another, several Circuit Courts of Appeal have held that the compulsory license provision of the federal copyright law does not entitle record pirates to duplicate uncopyrighted sound recordings. *E.g., Edward B. Marks Music Corp. v. Colorado Mag., Inc.*, 497 F.2d 285 (10th Cir. 1974), *appeal pending*, 95 S.C. 36 (1975); *Duchess Music Corp. v. Rosner*, 458 F.2d 1305 (9th Cir. 1972), *cert. denied*, 409 U.S. 847 (1972).

Difficulties with such a crime spread to the area of state anti-piracy laws for two reasons. For one, the crime of *unauthorized duplication per se* (copying) and the crime of *infringement of a musical copyright via unauthorized duplication* (infringement-via-copying) appear to present a problem of merger. For another, it is difficult to reconcile any such merger with the impact, though not the facts, of *Goldstein v. California*, 412 U.S. 556 (1973).

Approaching discussion notes that *Goldstein* allows the states to deal with record piracy by employing state anti-piracy laws which protect against *unauthorized duplication*. *See* text accompanying notes 233-235 *infra*. Approaching discussion also notes the strong implication in *Goldstein* that the states may protect from illicit copying only those recordings which the federal copyright law does not protect from copying. *See* note 128 *infra* and accompanying text. However, if the federal copyright law allows prosecution and conviction of record pirates for a crime of infringement-via-copying, then the federal copyright law may be used in federal criminal enforcement against any type of record piracy, whether the piracy involves copyrighted or uncopyrighted sound recordings. Yet, if that is so, *and* the preclusive implication in *Goldstein* is a valid one, *and* copying and infringement-via-copying are to be considered a merged crime, then the states are effectively precluded from applying state anti-piracy laws to all post-Oct. 15, 1971 acts of record piracy. Since *Goldstein* involved a state conviction for acts of record piracy which were not only pre-Feb. 15, 1972 but also pre-Oct. 15, 1971, the case on its facts can be harmonized with (1) the viability of a federal crime of infringement-via-copying, (2) the preclusive implication in *Goldstein*, and (3) a merger of the

Recording Act. Congress did so because the film soundtrack was perceived to be already covered by another criminal liability net—the one which had long been in the Copyright Act to protect motion picture copyrights, among other copyrights, from infringement.[232]

In June of 1973, a third net of criminal liability relative to record piracy was authorized. That authorization, of course, came by way of the United States Supreme Court's decision in *Goldstein v. California*.[233] The *Goldstein* case involved a California record pirate who had been convicted under a California anti-piracy law which made unauthorized duplication a state crime.[234] The defendant sought to have that law and his conviction

---

crime of copying and the crime of infringement-via-copying. Such a harmonization, however, breeds the unsettling consequence of presently denying the states *any* power to protect against record piracy, since the statute of limitations has run on pre-Oct. 15, 1971 acts of record piracy.

On the other hand, if *Goldstein* is to be taken as a continuing sanction of present state anti-piracy laws which protect against the copying crime, *and* if the preclusive implication in *Goldstein* is a valid one, then the crime of copying and the crime of infringement-via-copying must be considered separate and distinct crimes. This consideration breeds the strange consequence that one class of record piracy actions (involving copyrighted recordings) is amenable to federal conviction for two crimes, each of which carries different penalties under section 104(a)&(b), while another class of record piracy actions (involving uncopyrighted recordings) is amenable simultaneously to state conviction for the crime of copying and to federal conviction for the crime of infringement-via-copying.

Whatever the case, inevitably we shall have answers as to which case is law and how that case can be law. The Justice Department has recently decided to supplement its prosecutions of the copying crime (under section 104(b)) with prosecutions of the infringement-via-copying crime (under section 104(a)). *See Justice Dept. To Step Up War Vrs. Pirates, U.S. Atty. Tells NARM*, Variety, March 12, 1975, at 61, col. 6. Meanwhile, prosecutions and convictions for the copying crime proceed at the state level under state anti-piracy laws in those cases where federal authorities cannot apply federal copyright law to copying *per se,* though in the same cases they may very well be able to apply federal copyright law to a crime of infringement-via-copying.

If both processions are permissible, *and* if the implication in *Goldstein* is valid, then *unauthorized duplication* and *infringement of a musical copyright via unauthorized duplication* must be deemed separate and distinct crimes. In that case we may note that even if *a* federal criminal copyright law may be used against *any* record pirate, jurisdiction over recording piracy remains dichotomous with regard to the crime of copying. Approaching discussion explores both this dichotomy in its initial posture and the degree to which such a dichotomy fades when the eclectically illegal product of soundtrack piracy is examined. *See* text accompanying notes 239-40 *infra.*

[232] *See* text accompanying notes 35-37 *supra.*
[233] 412 U.S. 556 (1973).
[234] CAL. PENAL CODE §653(h).

thereunder overturned as unconstitutional. In a 5/4 decision, the Court held that the area of copyright law was not an exclusively federal concern which disallowed state action in protecting record companies and music publishers. Instead, ruled the Court, the states were free to deal with record piracy by employing state anti-piracy criminal laws;[235] hence, the state anti-piracy law and the criminal conviction thereunder were upheld as constitutional.

California had adopted its anti-piracy statute in 1967, following the lead set by New York in 1966.[236] Several other states had passed anti-piracy laws before or while *Goldstein* was in the judicial process, on its way to the nation's highest court. The Court's decision in *Goldstein* not only sanctioned these state actions; it invited more states to pick up the gauntlet spread by the nation's record and tape pirates. New York and California—the major bases of organized soundtrack piracy if not of organized record piracy itself—have now been joined in their anti-piracy posture by thirty-six other states. Some of these states—including California—provide felony sanctions in the area of record piracy. Legislative movement along the state anti-piracy route is predicted for those states which have not yet adopted their own anti-piracy laws.[237]

It is not absolutely clear whether these state laws afford protection against all pirated, bootlegged, or counterfeited recordings, or whether they protect from unauthorized duplication only those recordings which the federal copyright law does not protect from unauthorized duplication *per se*. The Court in *Goldstein,* though it did not consider the issue directly, strongly implied that the states may protect from unauthorized duplication those recordings which the federal copyright law does not protect from unauthorized duplication.[238]

---

[235] The *Goldstein* ruling operates at least with respect to recordings fixed prior to February 15, 1972. No question was raised in *Goldstein* as to the power of the states to protect recordings fixed after that date. 412 U.S. at 552 n.7. *But see* note 238 *infra* and accompanying text *infra*.

[236] N.Y. PENAL LAW §441(c).

[237] *Justice Dept. To Step Up War Vrs. Pirates, U.S. Atty. Tells NARM,* Variety, March 12, 1975, at 61, col. 5.

[238] The Court ended its opinion in *Goldstein* by declaring, at 412 U.S. at 571 (emphasis added):

> *Until and unless* Congress takes further action with respect to recordings fixed prior to February 15, 1972, the California statute may be enforced against acts of piracy such as those which occurred in the present case.

Accord, Goldstein, *Inconsistent Premises and the Acceptable Middle Ground: A Comment on Goldstein v. California,* 21 BULL. CR. SOC. 25, 27 (1973); *The Supreme Court, 1972 Term–Patent and Copyright Law,* 87 HARV. L. REV. 282, n.5 (1973).

If this is indeed the case, then a record pirate in most areas of the United States may be identified as violating a criminal law which protects against unauthorized duplication—but he will commit that crime either under federal law or under a state law, depending upon the exact identity of the recording he appropriates. To this general rule born of the holding and implication of *Goldstein* there is, however, one salient exception: a record pirate who happens to engage in soundtrack piracy may bring his illegal activity under the concurrent purviews of federal *and* state criminal laws which protect against unauthorized duplication.

Reference was made earlier to the fact that the soundtrack pirate's product sometimes bears features which establish an eclectic illegality. If, for instance, a record pirate duplicates a legitimate recording which was "fixed" prior to the effective date of the Sound Recording Act, it is generally the case that he is immune from federal criminal liability as regards the crime of unauthorized duplication; as to that crime, only the state criminal laws may be used against this pirate within the criminal sphere.[239] If, however, a soundtrack pirate duplicates a legitimate recording which was "fixed" prior to the effective date of the Sound Recording Act, but that legitimate recording happens to be a soundtrack album upon which were "fixed" excerpts drawn by direct transfer from the music tracks of a motion picture, then the pirate's criminal liability posture, as to his unauthorized duplication, operates as a function of his violation of a motion picture copyright. The federal criminal law may be applied to this violation, in the same manner as the federal law would be applied had the appropriated music tracks not been licensed to a legitimate record company but bootlegged by the soundtrack pirate.

Further, if a soundtrack pirate duplicates a legitimate recording which was "fixed" prior to the effective date of the Sound Recording Act, and that legitimate recording happens to contain a mixture of direct transfer quotations from the music tracks of a motion picture and rerecorded quotations from the same motion picture score, then the pirate's criminal liability posture, as to his unauthorized duplication, operates both as a function of his violation of a motion picture copyright *and* as a function of his violation of an applicable state anti-piracy law. In this instance, the soundtrack pirate, with one illegal product, has violated the federal criminal law protecting the motion picture *and* the state criminal law protecting sound recordings issued before the sound recording amendment was enacted. These separate laws apply with equal force to the illegally duplicated product because the excerpts contained on the product bear separate legal identities, just as they would if the soundtrack

---

[239] *See* note 231 *supra*.

pirate *bootlegged* music tracks from one motion picture on one side of his product while he *pirated* rerecorded material from another motion picture on the other side of his product.

We may note, therefore, that the dimensions of the criminal liability network relative to organized soundtrack piracy operate as a function of a "bouncing ball" technical analysis of illicit soundtrack product where the crime of unauthorized duplication is concerned. Such a technical analysis is mandated before law enforcement authorities move against organized soundtrack piracy on an unauthorized duplication charge, because if different or dual criminal liability nets apply to this crime, then different or dual law enforcement authorities carry the power to move against an isolated instance of organized soundtrack piracy upon a charge of this crime. Since the "bouncing ball" technical analysis must be deemed at least initially confusing to those unfamiliar with the reasons why it is required, and since the emphasis in the area of enforcement of anti-piracy laws has so far been on enforcement of unauthorized duplication laws,[240] it is small wonder that organized soundtrack piracy has thus far been granted a full de facto immunity within the war on record piracy.

A number of examples suffice to demonstrate how the "bouncing ball" technical analysis might be applied in the enforcement of unauthorized duplication laws relative to organized soundtrack piracy. "Curtain Calls Records"—the largest soundtrack piracy organization operating in the United States—builds its catalog mostly by appropriating the original music tracks of copyrighted motion pictures, primarily musicals of the 1930s and 1940s. "Curtain Calls" operates from a base in New York. At the same time, an off-shoot soundtrack piracy organization operating from California devotes its activities wholly to counterfeiting the original "Curtain Calls" records, which are bootlegged discs to begin with. The internal pirate war is based on price positions: "Curtain Calls"-New York invades the market first with products selling at an $8 to $15 range, and "Curtain Calls"-California follows soon after with counterfeit/bootleg discs selling at a $5 level. Now, both New York and California have anti-piracy criminal laws which protect against unauthorized duplication. But "Curtain Calls"-New York and "Curtain Calls"-California deal only in illicit recordings which carry original motion picture music track transfers. If the jurisdictional dichotomy implicated by *Goldstein* is a valid one, then the activities of "Curtain Calls"-New York and "Curtain Calls"-California are solely a federal criminal concern.

Both "Cinema Records" and "Sound/Stage Recordings" operate otherwise, however, and so their posture in law emerges differently. Both

---

[240] *See* note 231 *supra.*

soundtrack piracy organizations offer titles in their catalogs which may be identified solely as bootlegged recordings of motion picture music tracks—a federal criminal concern. Both organizations also offer titles in their catalogs which may be identified solely as pirated recordings of legitimate label rerecordings of excerpts from one or more motion picture scores—a state criminal concern. Further, both organizations offer titles in their catalogs which may be identified as pirate/bootleg recordings: these combine pirated rerecorded film music quotations (the state criminal concern) and bootlegged direct transfer quotations from film soundtracks (the federal criminal concern). Irrespective of the validity of the jurisdictional dichotomy implicated by *Goldstein*, both the federal and the state law enforcement authorities may move against such organizations upon a charge of unauthorized duplication. That is, the twin moves may be made as long as the illicit product produced by such organizations is carefully targeted so that the varying legal identities born by different products do not conflict with either or both of the two jurisdictional nets which may be cast.

There is more to organized soundtrack piracy than manufacture and sale to mandate the attention of law enforcement authorities. There is also the element of distribution. Just as the manufacture/sale element of soundtrack piracy occupies a unique legal position within the general field of record piracy, producing an unusual vulnerability to the applied force of law once the avenues by which that force may proceed are carefully weighed, so the distribution/sale element of soundtrack piracy—operating at the retail store or mail-order level—may be clearly distinguished from that distribution/sale element which inheres in general record piracy itself.

The distinctions in this case are two-fold. First, and correlatively, the distribution/sale element of soundtrack piracy is subject to the same "bouncing ball" technical analysis as is the manufacture/sale element. If the distributors aid or abet infringements of copyright which the federal law protects against, then their liability is a federal concern. When their actions relate to infringing articles which the state laws protect against, then their liability is a state concern. And when, by their actions, the distributors come within the twin ambits of both federal and state law, then their liability emerges as dual as does the liability of their suppliers.[241]

---

[241] The issue of possible liability of the distribution/sale element as to aiding or abetting the commission of more than one crime is believed to be beyond the scope of the present analysis. *See* note 231 *supra.*

Second, and perhaps more importantly, the marketing characteristics which distinguish the distribution network which operates in the soundtrack market from the distribution network which operates in the overall record market, also establish the former network as much more vulnerable to the force of law—in the practical sense of enforcement—than is the latter network. As is well known, the aiding or abetting provision of the federal copyright law has very rarely been applied against retail distributors who sell pirate, bootleg, or counterfeit recordings from their inventories of such articles.[242] There is little mystery about this lapse, for the logic of the prosecutorial abstinence in this area is a simple and practical one.

To establish criminal liability on the part of retail distributors of infringing articles under the federal copyright law, it apparently is not necessary to prove that one charged with aiding or abetting a copyright infringement did so for profit, so long as the infringer aided or abetted was infringing a copyright for profit.[243] It is necessary, however, to prove that the aiding or abetting was knowingly and willfully done.[244] Equivalent "knowledge" requisites are also included in the state anti-piracy laws which outlaw distribution of pirate, bootleg, and counterfeit recordings.[245]

"Knowledge" at the distribution/sale level of record piracy is difficult to prove before a jury. For one, the penal provision must be strictly construed against the prosecution and in favor of the defendant.[246] For another, when a distributor handles thousands of record titles, released on scores of labels, and containing a dozen broad classes of recorded music, he is able to claim that he can hardly be expected to be intimately aware of, or even generally knowledgeable about, each and every article he sells—including those which are illegal. Whether or not they are uniformly honest, the distributors' claims of ignorance in the area of

---

[242] 2 M. NIMMER, NIMMER ON COPYRIGHT 709 (rev. ed. 1974). *See also Feds In Frisco Zero In On Disk Retailers To Head Off Pirates,* Variety, Feb. 26, 1975, at 49, col. 6.
[243] NIMMER, *supra* note 242, at 708 n.9.
[244] *See* note 223 *supra.*
[245] *E.g.,* N.Y. PENAL LAW §441(c) reads in appropriate part:
Any person who:
. . . .
(2) Shall sell any [pirate, bootleg, or counterfeit recording] with the knowledge that the sounds thereon have been so transferred thereon without the consent of the owner,
Shall be guilty of a misdemeanor.
[246] NIMMER, *supra* note 242, at 708.

record piracy have been uniformly persuasive enough to discount criminal prosecution.[247] Thus, since the burden of proof carried by prosecutorial forces generally looms as insurmountable so as to remove the threat of prosecution from the activities of retail distributors, these distributors generally enjoy a de facto immunity which the manufacture/sale element generally does not enjoy.

However, the distribution/sale element which operates in the soundtrack market operates therein in a fashion which, by its peculiar marketing distinctions, excludes all benefit of the cloak of practical immunity worn by other record distributors. The stock-in-trade of this element happens to be rare soundtrack albums. The soundtrack market distributor, whether he operates by use of the mails, a store, or both, must know every title released, every label, every cover design, every market price, and every dimension of rarity relative to several hundred out of print legitimate soundtrack albums so as not to incur any opportunity loss in his elected specialty. "Knowledge" becomes something other than an insurmountable burden of proof when a specialty distributor sells the legitimate Capitol soundtrack album of "The Pride and the Passion" for $50 and its pirated counterpart for $5. This is even more the case when the distributor's widely circulated sales literature informs his consumers that pirate soundtrack albums do not adversely affect the market prices of their legitimate antecedents, and that all bootleg soundtrack albums listed for sale have indeed been produced by employing the original music tracks of the films which bear their titles.

The distribution/sale element of soundtrack piracy rises to a higher level of practical legal vulnerability when it participates in the consortium style of soundtrack piracy. As was seen earlier, consortium-style soundtrack piracy can only work when its operation is made very public. Here, the public must be informed directly by the distribution/sale element of its posture of aware assistance, in order that the tail which secures capital by brochure solicitation may wag the dog supplied with capital to commit an act of soundtrack piracy. We may note, then, that if it is the manufacture/sale element of organized soundtrack piracy which has been most prominent in defying both federal and state law enforcement authorities to bear the inconvenience of analysis and application of copyright law, it is the distribution/sale element of that piracy which has been mailing out the invitations.

---

[247] *See Blues Over Bootleg Record Boom Here,* N.Y. Post, Jan. 4, 1975, at 2, col. 3. *But see Feds In Frisco Zero In On Disk Retailers To Head Off Pirates,* Variety, Feb. 26, 1975, at 49, col. 6.

Finally, the practical legal vulnerability of the distribution/sale element of organized soundtrack piracy may be identified as most pronounced when the distribution/sale element and the manufacture/sale element are one and the same. This occurs in the case of an integrated soundtrack piracy organization, where the manufacturer employs its own mail-order and/or retail store network to achieve distribution. Here, "knowledge" may simply be deemed an implicit function of the integrated marketing activities.

CONCLUSION

Few developments in the history of motion picture copyright concerns have been more unfortunately bred than the promulgation of anti-protectionist theory with regard to the motion picture soundtrack. Nor have many developments in that history been more strangely sanctioned than the appearance and widening of a mini-industry devoted to seizing and marketing that which anti-protectionist theory would largely free into the public domain. The consummate challenge produced by these twin developments cannot be ignored. If the motion picture soundtrack is not protected by motion picture copyright, then we are living within the biggest musical and literary public domain ever accidentally bequeathed by the twentieth century entertainment industry. Yet if the motion picture soundtrack is protected by motion picture copyright, then we are tolerating, and encouraging by catatonic reaction, an economic climate of burgeoning criminal assault upon motion picture property, as to which protection in law must inevitably assume the mantle of meaningless formality.

Both in legal theory and in economic practice, these lines of conflict have not so much been drawn as they have been imposed. If they are not to multiply, they must be attended to in legal fashion. Where they are tolerable at all, intellectual mischief and economic mischief are tolerable only up to the point where they feed or feed off of each other. The impact of their appointed union places the societal importance of that appointment squarely in legal focus. For the reckoning invited, if it awaits at all, lies in law.

If such challenge must be met, the meeting must follow irrespective of any attending embarrassments. The argument which emerges from the present analysis is not only that anti-protectionist theory is wrong in its conclusions, but that it is also defective in its legislative assumptions, imprecise and often incorrect in its historical references, objectionable in its predicate analytical maneuvers, ignorant in its aesthetic awareness,

CONCLUSION

misinformed as to the seriousness of its pursuit, and altogether insupportable in law.

Still, it has not only been born in the commentaries, it has sprung therein as fully matured and as insistently armored as we are likely to see it stand. Until the status of the motion picture soundtrack within copyright law is judicially settled, the challenge presented by anti-protectionist theory will have to be met where the roots of the great motion picture soundtrack robbery have been planted: in the commentaries. Here, anti-protectionist theory should speedily be returned to its proper position in copyright law, stamped with the label of dangerous legal mythology. Here also, the protectionist theory urged by Professor Nimmer should be returned to a position of legal orthodoxy. As the preceding analysis evidences, whether the protection of the motion picture soundtrack be deemed an objective correlative of the legislative intent attending the express statutory recognition of motion picture copyright, or whether it be identified as a function of applying "species of the genus" analysis to the soundtrack copyrightability issue, Professor Nimmer's protectionist summary states the only conclusion that a necessarily wide-ranging investigation of law will support.

It might be argued, independently of substantive analysis, that the courts would not look with favor upon the prospect of a huge and sudden artistic anarchy in the area of motion picture property, and that therefore the courts would not allow such a result to flow. It might be more saliently contended, in accord with substantive analysis, that the courts would never plunge the motion picture industry into so fracturing a chaos as the judicial adoption of anti-protectionist theory would provide, when the case law, the legal authorities, the extra-judicial administrative positions, and an examination of legislative intent argue overwhelmingly on behalf of motion picture soundtrack protection. Either of these perceptions might be very sound, and yet they are insufficient as notations with which to lay the issue of soundtrack protection to analytical rest. The final embarrassment which inheres in the matters we have explored is that a criminally parasitic industry, much beyond the budding state, has been allowed to defy so many copyright laws, to operate so openly and profitably, to grow so quickly, and to present so substantial and continuing a threat to motion picture property and to the viability of penal copyright laws, without incurring any opposition.

As we have seen, a catatonic response to such an assault on motion picture property has not been without some justification. Apart from the fears fired by the promotion of anti-protectionist theory, the manner in which enforcement of law may proceed in this area is multi-dimensional and often confusing. An attempt has been made here to identify the pitfalls which exist in this area. A guide has been provided by which travel may progress through the maze of eclectically illegal product, functionally applicable law, isolated and concurrent jurisdictional networks, and practical barriers or vulnerabilities attending problems of proof. An excuse for prolonged inaction in opposing the physical dimension of the assault upon motion picture property no longer will lie. Unlike the cause of mitigating mere intellectual damage, the eradication of continuing economic damage cannot be made a reality in the commentaries alone. That is first and foremost the charge of the federal law enforcement agency, for it is at the federal level where protection of the motion picture soundtrack began, and it is at that level where that protection remains to be frontally enforced and finally sustained.

GLOSSARY OF LEGAL TERMS

a priori reasoning—This is reasoning which assumes a logical connection between one rule (as cause) and another rule (as effect). No investigation of how and why the "cause" rule produces the "effect" rule is involved.

amicus curiae brief—This is a brief introduced by a "friend of the court" during a judicial proceeding. This "friend of the court" is not directly involved with the legal proceeding which is underway. However, since his interests stand to be affected by a judgment against a party who *is* directly involved in the proceeding, the court may allow this collaterally interested party to argue on behalf of his own interests.

de minimis rules—These are requirements that minimal standards be met before the law will take notice of a legal status or a legal right. These standards vary with the legal context in which they are demanded. In copyright law, for instance, an author must meet certain minimal standards of original authorship before his work will be copyrightable (*e.g.*, titles, slogans, single statements, etc., are not copyrightable).

dictum, short for *obiter dictum*—This is anything a court says which is not essential to the decision of a case upon which the court is ruling in its opinion. Dictum may be analyzed by later courts for its logic and rightness, but it may not be given the weight of judge-made law until it actually becomes just that in a later case.

knowledge—This is the classic requirement of *scienter* in criminal law: that one committing a criminal act knew the nature of the act he was committing. In this context, "knowledge" does *not* mean that the actor knows what the law says about his act, since everyone is presumed to know the law. For example, if a person is charged with the crime of selling stolen property, the required "knowledge" is that he knew he was selling stolen property—not that he knew that selling stolen property was a crime.

licensee—This is a person (or corporation, partnership, etc.) who has a license to do a particular thing. It is a legal right, often purchased from one who has the right to sell this license to do a particular thing.

merger problem—This problem arises when a person has committed an act which fits within the definition of more than one crime. If the elements of one crime include all the elements of the other crime(s), the lesser crime(s) is said to "merge" in the greater crime. The result of this merger is that the perpetrator of the act may then be found guilty of only the greater crime. However, if any element of the lesser crime(s) is not an element of the greater crime, the perpetrator of the act may be found guilty of multiple crimes growing out of one act. Weighing the merger problem therefore involves a careful analysis of the elements of each crime embraced by the criminal act.

standing—This is the power of a private party to take legal action in a particular situation. For instance, to have standing to sue a party who has committed a wrong, one must show that one's *personal* right has been infringed by the party who has committed the wrong. If the right infringed belongs, in fact, to a third party, then only this third party has standing to sue the party who has committed the wrong.

statute of limitations—This is a statute which sets forth a time limit within which an indictment must be filed (in a criminal action) or a lawsuit must be begun (in a civil action) after a crime, or an event which establishes the right to sue, has taken place. A wide variety of federal and state statutes of limitations set forth a wide variety of time periods in which a wide variety of crimes and civil causes of action must be acted upon if they are to be acted upon at all.

sui generis treatment—This is treatment peculiar to one class. It is often deemed necessary because of an oversight made in writing a statute to cover different classes.

TABLE OF CASES

American Mutoscope & Biograph Co. v. Edison Mfg. Co., 137 Fed. 262 (C.C.D.N.J. 1905)......35–37,40,42,44–46
Blanc v. Lantz, 83 U.S.P.Q. 137 (Cal. Super. Ct. 1949)......13
Brandon Films v. Arjay Enterprises, 33 Misc. 2d 794, 230 N.Y.S. 2d 56 (1962)......13
Buck v. Jewell-LaSalle Realty Co., 283 U.S. 191 (1931)......39–41
Burrow-Giles Lithographic Co. v. Sarony, 111 U.S. 53 (1884)......35, 44–46, 48, 71–72
Duchess Music Corp. v. Rosner, 458 F.2d 1305 (9th Cir. 1972), cert. denied, 409 U.S. 847 (1972)......94
Edison v. Lubin, 122 Fed. 240 (3d Cir. 1903)......17–18, 34–37, 40, 42–46
Edward B. Marks Music Corp. v. Colorado Mag., Inc., 497 F.2d 285 (10th Cir. 1974), appeal pending, 95 S.C. 36 (1975)......94
Encore Music Publications, Inc. v. London Film Productions, Inc., 89 U.S.P.Q. 501 (S.D.N.Y. 1951)......22
Foreign & Domestic Music Corp. v. Licht, 196 F.2d 627 (2d Cir. 1952)......22
Goldstein v. California, 412 U.S. 546 (1973)......5, 94–99
Jerome v. Twentieth Century Fox-Film Corp., 67 F. Supp. 736 (S.D.N.Y. 1946), aff'd, 165 F.2d 784 (2d Cir. 1948)......9, 35–37
Jerome H. Remick & Co. v. American Automobile Accessories Co., 5 F.2d 411 (6th Cir. 1925)......39–40
Jewelers' Circular Pub. Co. v. Keystone Pub. Co., 274 Fed. 932 (S.D.N.Y. 1921)......45
Jewelers' Mercantile Agency Ltd. v. Jewelers' Weekly Pub. Co., 155 N.Y. 241, 49 N.E. 872 (1898)......13
Kalem Co. v. Harper Bros., 222 U.S. 55 (1911)......9, 38–41
L.C. Page v. Fox Film Corp. 83 F.2d 196 (2d Cir. 1936)......8–9, 15, 17, 34–38
Metro-Goldwyn-Mayer Distributing Corp. v. Bijou Theatre Co., 59 F.2d 70 (1st Cir. 1932)......41–42
Metro-Goldwyn-Mayer Distributing Corp. v. Bijou Theatre Co., 17 U.S.P.Q. 124 (D.C. Mass. 1933)......41
Pagano v. Chas. Beseler Co., 234 Fed. 963 (S.D.N.Y. 1916)......45
Patterson v. Century Productions, Inc., 93 F.2d 489 (2d Cir. 1937), cert. denied, 303 U.S. 655 (1938)......13
Reiss v. National Quotation Bureau, Inc., 276 Fed. 717 (S.D.N.Y. 1921)......45–46, 48
Rossiter v. Hall, 20 Fed. Cas. 1253, No. 12,082 (C.C.E.D.N.Y. 1866)......38–40
Tiffany Productions, Inc. v. Dewing, 50 F.2d 911 (D. Md. 1931)......41
Universal Pictures Co., Inc. v. Harold Lloyd Corp., 162 F.2d 354 (9th Cir. 1947)......41

West v. Francis, 5 Barn. & Ald. 743......21
White-Smith Music Publishing Co. v. Apollo Co., 209 U.S. 1 (1908)......19–22, 24–25, 34, 47–48, 69, 71–73, 79–80
Wood v. Abbot, 30 Fed. Cas. 424, No. 17,938 (C.C.S.D.N.Y. 1866)......43

INDEX

ABA Committee on International Copyrights, 10–11
Alamo, The, 54, 66–67
Alexander Nevsky, 54
American Bar Association, 10–11
American Road, 82
Anderson, William, 76
Antheil, George, 76, 83
Arthur, Jean, 60
Assassination du Duc de Guise, L', 28
audiovisual works, 78
Bailey, J., 21
Bell Telephone Laboratories, 29
Ben-Hur, 61
Bernstein, Elmer, 7, 27, 50, 53, 56, 58, 61, 82–83
Bernstein, Leonard, 61
Best Years of Our Lives, The, 56
Birth of a Nation, 29
Bliss, Arthur, 83
Bogsch, Arpad, 77
Brandeis, Louis, 39–41
Bride of Frankenstein, The, 56
Brylawski, E. Fulton, 3, 9, 14, 16–17, 20–22, 32, 78–79
Caine Mutiny, The, 82
California anti-piracy law, 95–96, 98
Child Is Born, A, 82
"Cinema Records", 80–81, 89–99
Cinematograph, 26
cinematographic works, 10–11, 77–78
Citizen Kane, 51–52, 75
Cleopatra, 61
Cocteau, Jean, 53
compulsory license agreement, 22–24, 36–37, 92, 94
Conkling, Jim, 23
Considine, Shaun, 82
Cook, Page, 52, 58

Copland, Aaron, 83
Copyright Association of America, 10
Copyright Office,
    neutral position, 7, 13
    protectionist position, 13–15, 78
    rejection of lone soundtrack, 20–21, 78–79
Copyright Revision Bill, 78
criminal copyright laws,
    federal, 5, 92–101
    previous exception to, 92–94
    state, 5, 92–101
"Curtain Calls Records", 85, 89, 98
De Forest, Lee, 30
De Mille, Cecil B., 53
Dean, James, 60
Diary of Anne Frank, The, 67
Dickson, William, 25, 26
dramatico-musical compositions, 32–33
Dream Street, 29
dubbing, 6
East of Eden, 60
Eastman, George, 25
Edison, Thomas, 25–26, 28, 38
Eisenstein, Sergei, 76
Embler, Jeffrey, 53, 55, 57
Evans, Luther, 11
Exodus, 66–67
Farenheit 451, 62
film dialog tracks, 3–4, 6, 12, 18–19, 22, 46, 48, 58–75
film dramatic work, 6–7, 12, 17, 32–33, 41
film loops, 17, 26, 34–35
film music, 6–7, 12–15, 17, 22–23, 26–31, 36, 48–69, 74–75, 82–83
film music tracks, 3–4, 6, 12, 15, 19, 22, 46–48, 58, 75, 97

109

film sound effects, 26–27, 29, 54
film sound effects tracks, 6, 75
film visual track, 6, 12, 20–21, 31, 48, 74–77
Fisher, Arthur, 10
Ford, John, 60
"Foreign American Productions", 90
foreign films, 21, 79
Fox Films, 29–30
Friedhofer, Hugo, 56, 82–83
Gilling, Ted, 52–53, 55, 61, 68
Gold, Ernest, 6, 67, 82
Goldsmith, Jerry, 64, 82
Goldstein, Paul, 96
Grant, James Edward, 66
Griffith, D. W., 29, 49
Hand, Learned, 22, 45, 48, 64, 72
Harris, Julie, 60
Hawks, Howard, 51
Hendricks, Gordon, 51
Henry V, 54
Herrmann, Bernard, 52–53, 55, 61–62, 68, 82–83
Hitchcock, Alfred, 60–61
Holmes, Oliver Wendell, 72–73
Huntley, John, 27–29
Informer, The, 50
Jazz Singer, The, 30
Johnny Belinda, 60
Johnson, William, 49, 54
Jolson, Al, 30
Julius Caesar, 62–63
Kaper, Bronislau, 58, 76, 82–83
Keough, Austin, 11
Keziah, Dorothy Pennington, 13
Kinetoscope, 26
King Kong, 56, 62
Knight, Arthur, 26–27, 29–30, 49
Korngold, Erich Wolfgang, 59–60, 82–83
Korngold, George, 60
Latman, Alan, 7, 19, 32, 44, 68
Laura, 50
Lees, Gene, 85
Legion of Decency, 57
Limbacher, James, 26, 28–29, 51, 53, 55, 58, 60, 63, 76
Lindgren, Ernest, 53
Little Tich and His Big Boots, 27
Lumière Brothers, 26
Madame Bovary, 56
Magnificent Seven, The, 53, 56

mail-order soundtrack dealers, 88–91, 99, 101
Mancini, Henry, 82
Mankiewicz, Joseph, 61
Manvell, Roger, 27–29
Margolis, Garry, 86
Martin, Dean, 51
Massey, Raymond, 60
"material contribution/enhancement of enjoyment" theory, 18–19, 47–49, 68–69
Meagher, William, 34, 37, 40, 43
mechanical reproductions—*see,* sound recordings
Méliès, Georges, 27, 49
Moross, Jerome, 82
Motion Picture Industry Association of America, 84
motion picture industry practice, 4, 6–7, 9–11, 14–15, 22–23, 27–30, 32
MPAA Print Security Office, 84
Muybridge, Eadweard, 25
New York anti-piracy law, 96, 98, 100
Newman, Alfred, 56, 67, 82–83
Nimmer, Melville, 4, 7–8, 15–16, 19, 23, 100, 103
North, Alex, 15, 57, 61–62, 66, 68, 82
Nun's Story, The, 57
Olivier, Laurence, 54
On the Waterfront, 61–62
Palmer, Christopher, 52, 68
Papillon, 64
Phonofilm, 30
phonograph, 25–27
phonograph records—*see,* record albums
photograph, 17, 25, 31, 34–35, 38, 43–46, 72
"physical sameness" theory, 17, 35, 42–44
piracy,
    aiding or abetting of, 99–102
    consortium operation of, 89–91, 101
    criminal status of, 92–102
    film piracy, 84–95
    soundtrack piracy, 4, 80–81, 83–92, 94–95, 97–102
    record piracy, 4, 86, 93–101
Place In the Sun, A, 51
Previn, Andre, 82
Pride and the Passion, The, 101
Prokoviev, Sergei, 54, 83

INDEX

Psycho, 55
publication, 10–12, 15, 29, 31, 77, 78–79
Puget, Henri, 11
Quo Vadis, 65
Raksin, David, 51, 58, 82–83
"reasonableness" theory, 8–9, 16–19, 24–25, 33–48, 69–80, 103
record albums, 12–13, 15–16, 19, 21–23, 27, 29–30, 74, 81–83, 86–94, 96–97, 100–101
Red River, 62
registration,
 of published works, 7, 13–15, 29, 31, 78–79
 of unpublished works, 7–14
Ringer, Barbara, 13
Rio Bravo, 51
Rosenman, Leonard, 53, 54, 60, 63–64, 82–83
Rosenthal, Laurence, 58–59, 62
Rozsa, Miklos, 23, 56, 61, 63, 65, 82–83
Saint-Saëns, Camille, 28
Sarris, Andrew, 51
Schimel, Adolph, 10
Schumach, Murray, 57
Sea Hawk, The, 83
Selznick, David O., 23
Shostakovich, Dimitri, 83
"silent films", 16, 21, 25–33, 74, 79
Since You Went Away, 23
Sound Recording Act, 11–13, 20, 78, 92–95, 97
 legislative history of, 12, 78, 92–93
sound recordings, 12–13, 22–23, 36–37, 76, 92–96
"Sound/Stage Recordings", 80–81, 89, 98–99
Spartacus, 65–66
"species of the genus" theory, 8–9, 16–19, 21, 24–25, 33–48, 69–80, 103
Spellbound, 23
Stagecoach, 62
Steiner, Max, 23, 50, 56, 62, 82–83
Stevens, George, 67
Stewart, James, 60
Streetcar Named Desire, A, 51, 57
Sutak, Ken, 81
synchronization license, 22–23, 36

synesthesia, 76
Syracuse University's George Arents Research Library, 85
"talkies", 8–9, 16–17, 25–26, 29–30, 36–37
Tannenbaum, Samuel W., 10
Ten Commandments, The, 53
They Died With Their Boots On, 62
Thomas, Tony, 6, 49–50, 54, 56, 58, 64, 67–68, 76
Thomson, Virgil, 83
Tiomkin, Dimitri, 54–55, 60, 62, 66, 82–83
To Kill a Mockingbird, 56
Townsend Amendment, 8–10, 25, 30, 31–33, 36, 41, 43, 46–47
 legislative history of, 31–33, 37
UCC Inter-Governmental Copyright Committee, 10–11
Universal Copyright Convention, 77–78
 legislative history of, 9–11
Valenti, Jack, 84
Vaughan-Williams, Ralph, 49, 83
Vertigo, 61
Vidor, King, 49
Vitaphone, 29–30
Walton, William, 54, 76, 83
Warner Brothers, 29–30
Waxman, Franz, 51, 56–57, 82–83
Wayne, John, 51, 60
White-Smith "intelligibility" test, 20–21, 24–25, 34, 47–48, 71–80
White-Smith "visual appreciability" test, 20–21, 24–25, 34, 47–48, 71–80
What's the Matter With Helen?, 58
Who's Afraid of Virginia Woolf?, 62
Wick, Ted, 23
Wiley, Alexander, 10, 11
Winkler, Max, 28–30
Wuthering Heights, 56
Wyoming University's Division of Rare Books and Special Collections, 85
Yarnell, Jules, 4
Young, Victor, 82–83
Yuzek, Dean, 3, 6, 9, 13–15, 17–18, 20–22, 24, 47, 78–79
Zamecnik, J. S., 28
Zinnemann, Fred, 57